'*Think Like An Entrepreneur* is a rich, practical and well-crafted book. Bringing together principles and methods from NLP, transactional analysis and coaching, Robbie Steinhouse provides extremely useful tools and know-how, gathered from his own lif∈ experience that can help anyone navigate the journey of ᴉng a successful business. The book is easy to read, jargon- and filled with clear examples and exercises. *Think Like An* ᴐreneur is a wonderful guidebook for anyone who is ready ᴉrt their own business and begin living their dreams.'

ᴐrt Dilts, *Founder of NLP University and leading contributor to the field of NLP since the 1990s*

Steinhouse is an entrepreneur with a difference: he ᴨow he does it. He combines the best of real-word com- ᴉ acumen with some of the most cutting-edge personal ᴐpment tools on the planet. I love the style of this book ᴐnversational and transformational.'

Kimberley Hare, Co-Founder and CEO, Kaizen Training Limited

ᴉthoritative and sharply written guide to the psychology of ᴈs in business.'

ᴉarez, *Novelist, Poet, Critic and author of many highly praised non-fiction books including* The Biggest Game in Town

ploy yourself can be a step towards freedom. This book ᴈ you how to make dreams into reality - the world needs ᴉnds of dreamers.'

Jeanne Marine, actress and partner of Bob Geldof

ᴈterclass in the tools, techniques, behaviors and processes ᴉrning an idea into a successful business. A must read for all budding entrepreneurs.'

Suzan Barghash, Regional Director of HR Shared Services for Cargill

'*Think Like An Entrepreneur* gives you practical strategies for becoming a successful entrepreneur. If you have the desire, the passion and the will to do what it takes **now**, this book will show you how!'

Shelle Rose Charvet, author of Words That Change Minds: Mastering the Language of Influence

'Robbie Steinhouse is an inspirational tutor and mentor. He has an easy-going style and employs NLP techniques to get the very best out of you. Whether you are a budding entrepreneur or a veteran manager, this book gives you the best tools to start you off on a higher learning curve. A must-read book.'

Jimmy D. Contractor, Company Secretary, Tata Limited

'The difficult thing about being an entrepreneur is that it's all in your head.'

Vincent Tchenguiz - world-renowned entrepreneur

'Life is full of challenges, whether you are an artist, business person or wherever you are on your journey. The key however is to be able to embrace techniques to keep you moving forward and this book provides them in abundance.'

Eva Hamilton MBE, Founder, Warrior Programme

'You can't grow your business without growing your people. This book provides invaluable assistance in achieving both objectives.'

Nigel Bannister, Chief Executive, Peverel Limited

'Robbie Steinhouse is a great coach, and this book brings his expertise to life. It will instill entrepreneurship into any organization, regardless of its size.'

Diane Yates, Head of Learning Services, National Australia Bank

'Robbie Steinhouse has a great understanding of the entrepreneurial process, and Chris West has helped him put it across in his usual clear, amusing and jargon-free way.'

Mike Southon, author of The Beermat Entrepreneur

'Working with Robbie gave me the confidence and the frame of mind for the decision-making process. I very much look forward to working with his book and applying it to my entrepreneurial ventures.'

Allan Busse, Managing Partner, Ambiente LLP

'*Think Like An Entrepreneur* has been written by people that are practicing what they preach, a great book for those people wanting to understand and develop their communication skills and release their true potential.'

James Pritchard, Managing Director, JPA Group of Companies

'This book shines new light upon entrepreneurial ideas I thought I knew – and knew I thought. It is a partner in the lonely world of entrepreneurship. Demystifying, inspiring, rejuvenating!'

Bernie Wales, entrepreneur

'This is the sort of book that you'll reach for and read again and again: when you are starting out as an entrepreneur, again when you've started; again at your first set-back; and again when you've made it ... Despite its clear and easy to read format, there is so much wisdom and personal learning in here that you won't take it all in at once.'

Rebecca Klug, Director, Leading Service Ltd and former Controller of Heathrow Airport

Think Like An Entrepreneur

PEARSON
Prentice Hall
BUSINESS

Books that make you better

Books that make you better – that make you *be* better, *do* better, *feel* better. Whether you want to upgrade your personal skills or change your job, whether you want to improve your managerial style, become a more powerful communicator or be stimulated and inspired as you work.

Prentice Hall Business is leading the field with a new breed of skills, careers and development books. Books that are a cut above the mainstream – in topic, content and delivery – with an edge and verve that will make you better, with less effort.

Books that are as sharp and smart as you are.

Prentice Hall Business.
We work harder – so you don't have to.

For more details on products, and to contact us, visit
www.pearsoned.co.uk

Think Like An Entrepreneur

Your psychological toolkit for success

Robbie Steinhouse and Chris West

PEARSON

Prentice Hall

BUSINESS

Harlow, England • London • New York • Boston • San Francisco • Toronto • Sydney • Singapore • Hong Kong
Tokyo • Seoul • Taipei • New Delhi • Cape Town • Madrid • Mexico City • Amsterdam • Munich • Paris • Milan

PEARSON EDUCATION LIMITED

Edinburgh Gate
Harlow CM20 2JE
Tel: +44(0)1279 623623
Fax: +44(0)1279 431059
Website: www.pearson.co.uk

First published in Great Britain in 2008

f this work has been asserted by
s Act 1988.

sh Library

or success / Robbie Steinhouse

ISBN 978-0-273-71838-3
1. Entrepreneurship--Psychological aspects. 2. New business enterprises--Management.
I. West, Christopher, 1940- II. Title.
HB615.S733 2008
658.1'1--dc22
                              2008027324

10 9 8 7 6 5 4 3 2 1
12 11 10 09 08

Illustrations by Sarah Arnold

Typeset in 10/15pt IowanOldSt BT by 3
Printed and bound in Great Britain by Ashford Colour Press Ltd, Gosport, Hants

The publisher's policy is to use paper manufactured from sustainable forests.

Contents

Note from Robbie

I would like to dedicate this book to my father, Irwin (Terry) Steinhouse, who taught me how to make money and how to avoid it becoming your master.

I would also like to thank my many other teachers, some whom I have met and worked with, others whose inspiration has come simply via the written or spoken word (or, as in one of the people below, the rock-solid beat). I would especially like to mention Robert Dilts and Eric Berne. Robert both teaches and demonstrates that those who have a higher purpose can achieve things far beyond those with talent alone. He is an NLP father-figure (a youthful looking one) who has spread so much positive change across the world that NLP is finally getting the positive reputation it deserves. Eric was the founder of Transactional Analysis: like my father, he came from Montreal, loved poker and understood people in an amazing way. I would also like to thank Edward Hines, Connirae Andreas, John Bonham, Chen Man Ch'ing, Hilary Cochran, Ken Cohen, Stephen Covey, Judith Delozier, Ian McDermott, Wayne Dyer, Aina Egeberg, Jan Elfine, Milton Erickson, Lois Evans, Tony Felix, Stephen Gilligan, Joe Girard, Thich Nhat Hanh, Bill Hicks, John Peisley, Hyrum Smith, Suzi Smith, Mike Southon, James Sumerfield, Eckart Tolle, Alison Underwood and Ken Wilber.

Thanks, too, to Chris West, my co-author, who immersed himself as a client, student and craftsman in the material, ensuring that we came up with a truly easy-to-read NLP-orientated book – people familiar with the NLP genre will understand what an achievement this is! And finally, thank you to my family, friends, business partners and staff, to Ann Baldwin who has been a guiding light, and to the team at Pearson, especially our editor Samantha Jackson for guiding and trusting us to make this book.

All authors like to hear from readers: if you find this book helpful but want to ask further questions (or just comment), do get in touch. My email is Robbie@nlpschool.com. I look forward to hearing from you.

Robbie Steinhouse
London, May 2008

Introduction

"The difficult thing about being an entrepreneur is that it's all in your head."

Vincent Tchenguiz

In this book, I am taking you on a journey. It's about as exciting a journey as one can take – the journey of building a successful business.

As I'm going to be your guide on this journey, I should begin by introducing myself. I grew up in an entrepreneurial family, so I guess I've been studying how to think like an entrepreneur all my life. My family encouraged me to see the world in certain ways, that I thought were obvious but later on realised were actually quite unusual. Naturally as a young man I rebelled against this, and went out and did something totally unentrepreneurial – found a rather junior job in the City. That lasted a handful of months before it drove me crazy, then I went and got on with what I should have done from the beginning, starting my own business. The beliefs and values I bought with me made this move possible, but there was still a huge amount of learning to do – something you never stop doing if you are an entrepreneur.

As I built my business, I found myself being fascinated by the psychology of the people I came into contact with: customers, staff, competitors, fellow entrepreneurs ... So when the business was big enough to run without me – or, let's be honest, when it was better off running without me, as most successful enterprises outgrow their creators – I embarked on a serious study of human psychology. As a student, and later teacher, of NLP and TA (I'll explain these acronyms below), I discovered remarkable tools for understanding and changing people's mental states. I felt a strong need to put these tools to use in a commercial context, so founded an NLP school (NLP School Europe) and became a business coach. In the latter role, I found myself coaching many entrepreneurs; some just starting off, others massively successful (but still confused about the meaning and value of their success), others in the process of building businesses.

What did I learn from those experiences? All sorts of things, but I find it helpful to sort them into three categories. I intend to share all three kinds of thinking like an entrepreneur with you in this book.

At the most basic level, there are the *specific practical lessons* that we all learn as we build our businesses. These come from many sources: books, mentors, colleagues, rivals, but above all, experience. To continue the journey metaphor, these are the equivalent of maps, phrase books or guides containing travellers' 'tips' on where to get a good lunch or how to book a seat on a train.

Next, come those *beliefs and values* that entrepreneurs share, but which other people seem to lack. Without these, no amount of 'how-to' knowledge will ever be translated into actual wealth creation. I learnt many of these as a child, largely from my dad; other entrepreneurs born into unentrepreneurial families seem just to have them anyway; a third set of individuals acquire them later in life, often in an angry realisation that 'working for the man' for years hasn't really got them very far. In the journey metaphor, these are equivalent to in-depth knowledge about the culture, customs and history of the places we are going.

Finally, there are the *change processes*. The job of these is to get yourself fit for the rigours of the journey and to keep you fit as you undertake it. Even the most entrepreneurial of us start off with psychological 'baggage' that we need to ditch: fears, misconceptions, 'life scripts'. It's easy to reject these at an intellectual level, but this isn't enough when faced with the need to perform in the heat of the moment – a need that entrepreneurs face regularly – at which point people can easily relapse to their old selves. The 'Change Yourself' sections in this book are designed to give you a new set of habitual reactions, to make you think like an entrepreneur at the deepest level. 'Knowledge is only a rumour till it is in the muscle,' as they say in Papua New Guinea.

All three types of learning are essential to entrepreneurial success. How-to materials on their own remain theory; how-tos plus the right beliefs and values will get you underway, only to hit various brick walls as you build the business. But on the other hand, the most psychologically prepared individual needs to know what actually to do. Only with all three can you set off, act wisely and succeed.

How to use this book

Each chapter is structured in a similar fashion.

- I begin with some basic *'how-to' information*, gleaned from my experience as an entrepreneur or as a coach of other entrepreneurs.

- Then I introduce a particular new *concept* that I feel is useful at that particular point.

- Finally there is a 'Change Yourself' section containing a *self-coaching process* for which you will need time, a computer (or a pen and paper) and the preparedness to think new and possibly uncomfortable thoughts.

The 'how-to' parts of the book follow the journey of entrepreneurship, from starting out as a one-person band to leaving a large business 'on a high'. The change processes in each chapter are particularly appropriate to the phase of the journey described in that chapter – but they are also of value to entrepreneurs generally. I have coached many clients with large businesses using the processes in the beginning of this book; I have coached many clients who are just starting out using the processes at the end of the book. So, no matter where you are on this journey, read the whole book and do all the processes – they will all help you. If you are starting out, my aim is that when you have read the 'how-to' sections and done the processes, you will have both learnt and changed so much that you will feel like an experienced entrepreneur embarking on your second business.

Finally, note that all the processes can be done by yourself, but some can also be done with the help of a friend to act as your 'coach'. Your helper does not need specialist coaching skills to do this, but this person does need to be someone that you like and trust.

Three psychological systems

Psychology lies at the heart of this book, so I must introduce the three psychological systems whose influence is strongest in it (especially, but not purely, in the concepts and processes). This intro will be brief, though I hope that, as you work through the book, you become interested in the bodies of knowledge behind it and pursue that interest further. Doing so will be of huge use in your entrepreneurial careers, as business is ultimately about people: yourself, your colleagues, your customers . . .

NLP

NLP stands for Neuro-Linguistic Programming (NLP has an unfortunate liking for gobbledegook, which I do my best to deflate in this book). It is a set of tools for personal change and development. This makes it very different from most of the great psychological systems that arose during the last century, such as psychoanalysis or behaviourism, which sought to explain and systematise the entire human psyche. NLP has always taken a ruthlessly practical approach and claims to avoid deep theory. 'What works?' is its motto (a good motto for an entrepreneur, too!).

It began in California in the 1970s (no doubt a reason why some people dislike it). Its founders, Richard Bandler and John Grinder, were fascinated by expertise, especially in the field of therapy. They found three top therapists – Milton Erikson, Virginia Satir and Fritz Perls – and asked: 'Here are individuals who are clearly masters of their profession – what do they actually *do* that made them special?' (As Gregory Bateson, one of NLP's father-figures, put it, 'What is the difference that makes the difference?')

The obvious route, asking the experts directly, didn't seem to work: the experts' answers sounded a lot like the answers of other, much less successful therapists, and also contradicted each other. So Bandler and Grinder recorded therapy sessions, then went through the transcripts word-by-word, analysing what was actually said and done – a typical down-to-earth NLP approach. They noticed a set of patterns, a set of ways in which the therapists intervened to change the beliefs and attitudes of the patients. They codified these patterns into a model, then tested it to see if it worked. It did, and a new therapy was born.

NLP has since branched in many directions, developing new models and applying them to new areas. One area where it has been most useful is in business. It lies behind a lot of sales training. NLP thinkers have done modelling exercises, similar to the ones done on the therapists, on successful business people – for example Robert Dilts's 'Disney' model of creativity, based on an analysis of the practice of Walt Disney (Disney, don't forget, wasn't just a man who drew a cute mouse, but an entrepreneur who built one of the largest businesses in the world).

Over time, NLP has become a serious body of knowledge offering considerable insight into many aspects of life, both private and commercial. I have been involved in NLP for a long time, studying with some of the top practitioners in Britain and the USA. I believe strongly in its psychological depth, its relevance to business life and, most important of all, its power to change people.

TA

TA is otherwise known as Transactional Analysis. Like NLP, it is a therapeutic system that involves models of human behaviour and 'interventions' (tools for changing people).

TA's origins are much more orthodox than NLP's: its founder, Eric Berne, was a trained Freudian psychoanalyst. However, the system has not developed the momentum of NLP. It now takes many years of study to qualify in TA, and the results of TA therapy are, when tested objectively, not particularly impressive. Sceptics might say that this doesn't say much for the system, but this is unfair. NLP aimed at a less ambitious target, helping fundamentally sane people to grow and develop, while TA – like its parent, psychoanalysis – set out to slay a much darker, more powerful monster: that of madness. Arguably this has been a mistake.

Anyway, that's TA's problem. On its journey to – well, I'm not sure where – TA has developed some models of human behaviour and motivation that are wonderfully powerful in the gentler context of coaching entrepreneurs, and I shall present the best of them in this book.

Coaching

Business coaching is best seen as a mixture of sports coaching, therapy and consultancy.

Sports coaching is about goals and about performance. So is business coaching. Coaches follow a clear procedure: goals are set, the individual is assessed against those goals, then a programme of self-improvement is developed and maintained to ensure the individual gets from their current state to the desired one. This then has to be translated into actual performance – as a sports person or an entrepreneur, there's no point in being super-fit, armed with all the skills and tactically astute, if the moment you are called upon to act you fall apart mentally.

From therapy (particularly from the 'person-centred' therapy of Carl Rogers), coaching gets a focus on the client. Sports coaches will tell their clients what to do; psychological coaches do not – the client sets the agenda. Coaching also assumes that the client has all the 'resources' they need – the coach's role is essentially one of unblocking the barriers that clients have created between themselves and their own wisdom and abilities. As Timothy Gallway, author of *The Inner Game of Tennis*, puts it:

'performance = potential minus interference'.

Though hard-line Rogerian coaches frown on it, business coaches give advice – but only when asked. Hence the link to consultancy. If I have a client with a business problem to which I think I have an answer, I offer that answer. The client, of course, can choose to accept, question or reject it. The advice offered in this book is done in that spirit.

Concept: Your 'entrepreneurial chip'

7

This is a notion that will be running through the entire book – it is something that you will be developing as your entrepreneurship journey unfolds.

My dad was a successful entrepreneur. Towards the end of his life he suffered a series of strokes and was confined to hospital. He had so much neurological damage that he couldn't remember anything for any length of time. My stepmother used to come to the ward and explain business problems to him. He would listen, ask questions and then give very clear answers. The following day she would come back and say that she had followed his guidance, which had created a new issue she wanted advice upon – and he would look baffled. He had no memory of the previous day's conversation at all. She would have to tell the whole story again, and he would listen, ask the same sort of questions he'd asked the day before and come up with new, excellent advice. It was as if he had developed a kind of computer chip in his head for taking in information and making good decisions, that lived on when the memory of all specific content, past or present, was absent. Watching this at work was very upsetting, but oddly fascinating too.

I now see the same 'chip' in myself – business information comes in and I just turn it into decisions, without really thinking how. (In the language of learning theory, I have developed 'unconscious competence'.) This is of enormous value, as entrepreneurs have to make decisions quickly.

Entrepreneurs often tell us to 'trust your instinct'. I think this is a misleading metaphor, as instinct is something innate, like the craving that makes birds suddenly migrate; whereas the entrepreneurial chip is a learnt thing. But I know what they mean – the chip has been built up over years of experience, and is so automatic that it feels like an instinct.

All analogies are imperfect: what my father had in spades, what I have acquired, and what I will help you to build inside yourself, isn't a chip or an instinct but a set of skills that will become automatic. But I'm sticking with the chip metaphor. 'Thinking like an entrepreneur' is what the chip does, and what this book will help you to do.

Change Yourself: The permission pattern

This is a way of giving yourself permission to succeed. This may seem an odd notion, but many of us have a kind of inner 'parent' (a TA concept; more on this later) which can get in the way of action. This process will get it off your back. (Remember the *Inner Game of Tennis* formula: 'performance = potential minus interference'.)

1 Write down what you want permission to do as a simple statement of intent. 'I am going to start my own business.' 'It's time to go for it – now!' 'Tell my parents I'm going to do it my way.' Nothing complex.

2 Write down all the negative consequences if you do <u>not</u> put this statement into action. For example, 'I'll spend the rest of my life feeling I never reached my true potential'; 'I'll never have enough money'; 'I'll always be a doormat for other people.'

3 Write down all the positive consequences if you do not put this statement into action: 'As an employee, I get a regular wage'; 'Some of my current work is interesting'; 'It's secure.'

4 Work out how many of the things in step 3 above are 'must haves' and how many are just 'would likes'.

5 For the 'must haves', work out how you could get these benefits and also achieve your aim. As you read this book, you will find plenty of material to help with this stage.

6 Now, say to yourself in front of a mirror: 'I give myself permission to do x', where x is your statement of intent in (1)

above. Say this in a special way. 'I give myself permission to START MY OWN BUSINESS.' Emphasise the bit in capitals. As you say it, make eye contact with yourself and speak louder and clearer. This may feel a little odd, but you are actually doing a bit of NLP on yourself, sending yourself what is called an 'embedded command'.

7   How does that feel? If that does not feel enough, go back to step 4 and consider what else you need to do to satisfy your objections. Now repeat steps 5 and 6 and give yourself permission again. Repeat this process until you feel a *real energy surge*. Permission granted!

Sunita, a therapist, wanted to start her own practice. We went through this process several times, then she suddenly went bright red, smiled and said, 'Wow, it worked!' A few weeks later, the practice was open for business.

Getting started

How do you start a business? One answer is 'quickly'. Entrepreneurs practise the adage 'ready ... fire, aim!' So I'll begin by talking about how to do your first deal straight away and how to use that experience to teach yourself how to start and build your business. Although for many this may be counter-intuitive, I will then explain that is in fact the entrepreneurial learning strategy. However, entrepreneurship is not reckless, so I go on to explain how to build a consulting base: how to gather people and resources to help you with the many decisions you will have to make. Lastly, I present a change process based on the idea that you are a hero or heroine in the unfolding story of your life. Let's start by hearing from one of my heroes, Winston Churchill on the night he became Prime Minister in May 1940.

'As I went to bed at about 3 a.m., I was conscious of a profound sense of relief: at last I had the authority to give directions over the whole scene. I felt as if I were walking with destiny and all my past life had been but a preparation for this hour and for this trial. My warnings over the last six years had been so numerous, so detailed and were now so terribly vindicated, that no one could gainsay me. I could not be reproached either for making the war or with want of preparation for it. I thought I knew a good deal about it all and I was sure I should not fail. Therefore, although impatient for the morning, I slept soundly and had no need of cheering dreams. Facts are better than dreams.'

My first business idea was really rather clever. I was going to borrow money, invest it in carefully selected stocks and have a 'trailing 10 per cent stop-loss', which meant that I'd hold the stocks that went up and bail quickly out of the ones that fell. The 'trailing' stop-loss meant that if a stock went up then started falling, I'd automatically get out before I lost all the gain. With great pride, I told my dad about this, and waited for his response. He went bright red and said it was the biggest load of bull he'd heard in his life. 'So what do you recommend?' I replied, a little hurt. 'Just make some [expletive deleted] money!' came the reply.

He was, of course, right. I needed to get out there and start doing business, to find something people wanted and provide it. My first actual business was an employment agency. While working out exactly what business I wanted to build, I was working as a temp, programming. There seemed to be a lot of demand for us temporary staff, so I put an ad in a magazine I had noticed the other temp programmers really liked reading (*Private Eye*, not a computer mag), asking for people to send in their CVs. Several came in, so I phoned round large businesses offering these people's services. Some were taken on. They did a good job; everyone was happy; I was in business. I ran the agency for several years, and it helped me finance my really big business, in property.

Do a deal as quickly as possible

This advice is not original to me: most successful entrepreneurs will tell you that. But many new entrepreneurs still ignore it, preferring instead to write and rewrite long business plans, spend money on marketing or, most common, tinker with the product. The latter is a particular curse of technology businesses, especially ones founded by groups of technicians with little business experience. Such people will often hold back from selling a product because various bugs haven't been ironed out and because they don't want to have substandard stuff around 'with our name on it'. This is understandable, but will be fatal for most businesses.

So should you just pile into any business?

Well, that's better than sitting around daydreaming! But it's better still to have a quick but systematic think through the basics of what you are doing. Your idea must stack up in theory: it must have the potential to sustain you and itself. In the short term, you must have a view on how long it will take to get to the point where it will sustain you. In the long term, does it have the potential for growth beyond a one-person business? I call this quick-think the 'five-minute business plan'.

As a coach, I meet a lot of people what want to be coaches too, and want to do it full-time. Many of them haven't done a five-minute business plan. I ask how much they reckon they can get for a coaching session. Many look at the basic rate and reply 'about £50 an hour'. (Top coaches, of course, get many times more than that, but if people feel that £50 is their limit, then that will be their limit.) They can't see more than ten people a week – no coach can; it's exhausting, and you need to spend time on things like admin, marketing and keeping notes. So there's a maximum possible income of £500 a week, from which have to come premises, marketing costs, supervision, plus a share for the taxman.

Then there is also the issue of timing: if they have no business at the moment, it will take a while to get a decent client list. How is the person planning to support themselves in the meantime? (In practice, most successful coaches start with what Charles Handy calls a 'portfolio' approach, doing various jobs including coaching. It can take many years to make a living at only coaching.)

The long-term question about growth maybe doesn't matter to a potential coach – the business isn't 'scalable', but doesn't need to be.

By contrast the temp agency clearly was a winner, with low start-up costs, cash coming in quickly, enormous potential – and I was doing my temp work while starting it, so no problems about paying personal bills in the early days. All I had to do was make it work!

So your idea passes this theoretical test. Now test it in practice as soon as possible. Get someone to buy whatever you are offering.

The five-minute business plan

- When up and running, will the business sustain me?
- How long will it take me to get to this point?
- In the meantime, how will I survive?
- In the long term, is the business 'scalable' (can it grow beyond just me)?

If you have sufficient energy and belief in both yourself and the value that your 'offer' can add, you will find a buyer. And not only that, but the buyer will actually like both you and the offer. In all my businesses, when I started out I was selling something that I didn't understand terribly well. Nonetheless I always found someone to buy it, and that person was always happy with what they got. They felt that what I lacked in experience I made up for in enthusiasm and determination: there is nothing better than to be served by somebody who really values your business.

A good metaphor is the Beatles in their Hamburg days. You have two clubs you could go to. One features a very slick group of professional musicians who all play well but are getting bored with the material. The other has this rough-and-ready but talented group from England. Which would you choose? Personally, I'd go for the Beatles every time.

In my early 20s, I had a bank manager who lent me money to pay wages to a contractor I had employed in my agency. He said he knew my business was a bit basic but he was sure I would make it one day and he loved spotting stars early. There are many people who want to work with a rising star.

'Doing a deal' means, of course, getting out there and selling. Approaching early prospects with a new product can be scary, especially if you don't have much entrepreneurial experience.

Some people just say 'feel the fear and do it anyway' (to quote Susan Jeffers), but I find it more helpful to look at the fear first. Ask yourself out loud, as you sit by the phone, suddenly nervous about making a call: 'What is the worst thing that could happen?' Reply out loud.

- *'The person will say no.'* Probably. All salespeople learn that they have to 'kiss lots of frogs', most of which don't turn into princes. Can you turn the 'no' to your advantage by doing some market research? (I view all cold-calling as an exercise in research, anyway.) Ask, in a non-confrontational way, why the person is not interested. Sometimes you will get a useful conversation going (yes, and other times you won't!)

- *'The person will get angry.'* This is pretty unlikely. If, for some reason, they do, then they are the one with a problem, not you.

- *'The person will hate me, and tell everyone else what a jerk I am and thus ruin my reputation.'* This is, of course, ridiculous, but the unconscious often harbours absurd notions like this: flush it out of its lair and it will lose any power it might have.

Once you have established a worst possible, non-silly outcome, just ask yourself: 'So what?'

The reply may get silly again. 'This is the best opportunity I'll ever have to sell to this, the perfect client ... If I blow it, it's downhill from here.' Don't censor this reply: let it get silly, then question it. Best opportunity *ever*? *Perfect* client? *Doomed* to be downhill?

Clearing your mind of such guff – NLP calls them 'limiting beliefs' – is good entrepreneur training. There are always opportunities. No client is perfect; there'll always be more, probably much better than this one. No outcome is predetermined.

A more realistic 'sensible worst outcome' is a run of bad luck, a run of 'no's, with no feedback on why. This happens to all salespeople. The best solution to this is to take a break, then come back refreshed.

Feeling more positive? Good. In truth, even if you have given your fear a good working-over, you may still feel a touch of apprehension as you start dialling. Fine. Great actors and performers often have pre-stage nerves; they say it 'keeps them on their toes'. 'Feel the fear and do it anyway' is good advice *once you have done all you can to tackle the fear.*

As with many fears, there is a useful message behind it. By calling someone out of the blue, you are effectively demanding their time and attention. Respect that fact. I always start coldcalls with something like 'Hi, it's Robbie Steinhouse here of X Company. Is this a good time to take a couple of minutes to find out if you are interested in Y?' Asking permission to take up a small amount of their time usually gets a reluctant 'Yes, but only a couple of minutes' – which is all you need to make the initial contact and see if they are at least a theoretical prospect.

Of course, you may not have to cold-call to get your first deal. Many entrepreneurs start their businesses by working for a company, then switch to being self-employed and having that company as a first customer. This is a great place to start, though can be dangerous if it makes you complacent and stops you going out and widening your customer base. Other entrepreneurs start by selling to friends, or at least to people who know and trust them. Whatever your 'route' to your first sale, take it as quickly as possible.

Learning the entrepreneurial way

So, now you've got your first customer. Well done: now you can really call yourself an entrepreneur. The only difference between you and Richard Branson is – well, quite a lot, but you're on your way. It's time to start learning your business.

Entrepreneurs learn differently from other people; we practise what I call 'dynamic learning', while a lot of learning is essentially static.

Most people think that learning has to take time. You start by going to college and studying a subject for a couple of years to get the theory in place. Then it's time to go into the workplace and put that theory into practice, learning over time which bits of the theory don't apply to you (or are just plain wrong), plus various practical titbits that don't really fit into the big model but clearly work. After, say, five or six years you should have a good balance of theory and practice, and can start considering yourself something of an expert. After 10 years, you really are an expert. (There's actually an established concept called the '10 year rule': 40 hours a week for 10 years, it says, and you have mastered a field.)

Dynamic, entrepreneurial learning works in reverse. Go into business; glean advice from anywhere and everywhere; learn the rest by guessing, having a go, making mistakes and working it out. For most people in the UK (it's even worse across the Channel), this is counter-intuitive. We're told to go to school; be a good boy or girl; learn; and once we have learnt, to get a job. Entrepreneurs start by giving themselves a job, which then teaches them what they need to know.

When I decided to start running NLP courses, I was not an expert on NLP course management. I was fascinated by the topic, and the idea of running courses had passed the five-minute business plan test. I knew a subject-matter expert, so I asked him if he would teach the course. When he said yes, I put a date into my diary and booked a room in a conference centre. I then had a lot of learning to do – about pricing, about how to sell and market to this audience, about what was expected in terms of presentation and delegate support.

I thoroughly enjoyed this learning. I knew that there was enough time both to learn and do the basics (I booked the room five months in advance). We ran the course and it was a success. Behind the scenes, I made lots of organisational mistakes, from which I learnt. The next course ran much more smoothly. I am now a qualified NLP trainer myself, and our courses are among the best in the country.

Naturally I'm talking about learning entrepreneurship, not every craft or skill there is. I had to learn the NLP I ended up teaching by going on courses in the UK and America, by hours of practice, by ploughing through the often opaque works of people like Chomsky and Bateson. But this is theoretical learning. Running a business is essentially a practical affair, which you learn from having three things:

- confidence
- a rational approach
- a deadline.

Most practical learning follows a pattern, whereby we proceed from unconscious incompetence through conscious incompetence to conscious competence and finally unconscious competence. In other words:

1 We can't do it, but we mistakenly think it's easy.

2 We can't do it, and we know the fact.

3 We can do it adequately, but it takes all our effort and attention.

4 We do it well without conscious thought.

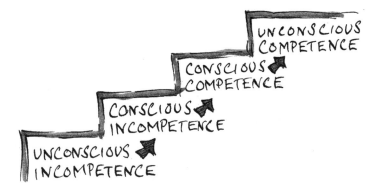

(This model is not from NLP or TA. Nobody knows exactly where it came from, though the most likely candidate is Noel Burch, an employee of Gordon Training International in the USA, back around 1970.)

Learning to ride a bike is a classic example of this pattern at work. When we're young, we see other children riding bicycles and think it's easy (unconscious incompetence). So we find a bike, get on, start pedalling, fall over and burst into tears (conscious incompetence). Children often say at this point 'I'll never do that!' But next day, they're usually out riding again. Soon they are competent, and putting all their effort into every aspect of their new-found skill – look at the face of a child at this stage of learning. Finally, of course, it's 'easy–peasy'. . .

Some people starting businesses give up at the falling over (conscious incompetence) point. Entrepreneurs find this a spur; they feel what psychologist Ellen Winner called a 'rage to master' the new topic, and won't rest till they have sorted out whatever made them fall.

Confusion is a natural response to the sudden onset of conscious incompetence. This can be painful, as it can catapult us back to childhood memories of not being able to do 'easy' things and feeling ashamed as a result. As an adult, learn to welcome confusion; it's a natural part of the learning process, not a signal that 'this is not for me'. Enjoy its 'open-endedness' – you aren't sure where this will lead, but your entrepreneurial chip will start telling you that it will be somewhere better than where you are now.

Building a consulting base

Part of dynamic learning involves 'gleaning advice from anywhere and everywhere'. This means building what I call a consulting base. By this, I don't mean a group of fresh MBA graduates whose organisations charge you several thousand pounds a day to tell you stuff you know already. I mean knowledgeable, experienced people to whom you turn for advice, and who give it generously and often free. (If it's not free, as it won't usually be from the legal or accountancy professions, then negotiate for it.)

It's useful to make a distinction between two types of advice: mentoring and 'tips'.

Get yourself a *mentor* as soon as you can. This particularly applies to people not brought up in entrepreneurial families. My dad was my mentor, and a wonderful one. When I started in business, I would call him most days. I would tell him what my current issues were, and his first question was often, 'What do you think you should do?' – a classic coaching intervention, allowing me to work things out myself. He would listen to my reply and either agree (which was reassuring) or suggest alternatives. He would only give actual advice ('Do this!') when he thought I was heading in totally the wrong direction.

Years later, after my dad had passed on, my business got into trouble and I found a mentor called Barry Pearson. Barry didn't know much about the property business, but he gave me my confidence back and reignited my determination to succeed, which was what I most needed at that time. He challenged very deep-seated insecurities in me in a robust way, and through the mentoring experience I became a stronger and better entrepreneur.

I have also had, and still have, mentors among my professional advisers. These include bank managers who had worked with lots of entrepreneurs, totally got the point of how we think and operate, and were happy to pass this knowledge on to me. (Bank managers are often portrayed as corporate robots, and some are. But don't assume that yours is, unless they show you they are.) My solicitor, Glenn Stevenson, has been a mentor for 20 years.

As I sit here writing, I can hear his voice, advising me 'Robert, sometimes the best thing to do, and the hardest thing to do, is to do nothing.' (Like many entrepreneurs, I have what TA calls a 'hurry-up driver', an inner voice that wants everything done yesterday.)

I get the best out of mentors at a 'high' level of input. By this I mean that they are most useful as sources of inspiration and positive attitudes, rather than basic 'how to do x' tips.

You do need basic 'how to do x' *tips* as well, of course. Become a kind of information magpie, shamelessly asking anyone and everyone for this kind of advice. Many experts are happy to provide it, aware that 'what goes around, comes around'.

A client of mine tells this story: 'When I first started out I didn't know anything about double entry bookkeeping. So I found an accountant in the Yellow Pages, called them up and asked them how to do it, and they explained it to me. They didn't charge me anything – though 20 years on, the same person is still my personal accountant.'

Using professionals

I've said that professional advisers can be mentors. Sadly, not all of them can, and some can be downright unhelpful. There are two problems with 'professionals'. One is that they can intimidate people with technical language; the other is that their attitudes are often too negative.

Intimidation first. The 'professions' tend to communicate with you in their own language, which they reckon it is up to you to understand. This is wrong. They should communicate with you in plain English. There are two reasons for this. One is simple good manners. The second is that if someone can only 'explain' a point by using gobbledegook, the chances are that they don't really understand what they are saying. You must interrogate lawyer- or accountant-speak until you are clear exactly what is meant by every word, phrase, clause, sentence or paragraph. If necessary, make a word-for-word translation. Don't just accept 'under the heretofore mentioned subsection the above named is permitted within reasonable authority to . . .' Establish exactly what the section means you can and can't do, and what other people can and can't do.

Second problem: negativity. Lawyers and accountants are cautious. That's their job, so I don't blame them for that. Their role is to look at all possible outcomes and protect their client – or, let's be honest, themselves. So they will be natural pessimists. Supposing X happens . . . Supposing Y happens . . .

Entrepreneurs cannot be like this. We have to be optimists. Rational, planning optimists, but optimists. So what do you do, given this clash? One answer is to avoid the professions altogether. This usually ends up badly. A much better option is to treat professional advice with a pinch of salt. A great question to ask lawyers and accountants is: 'What's the worst that could happen if I do this?' If the answer is catastrophic, then pay close attention to the advice. Often, however, the answer is trivial.

Rick, a property entrepreneur, says, 'I tell my lawyer, "Just do it!" If he gets really upset, then I figure out what the issue is and do something about it.'

Remember, the law is not black-and-white; it is a matter of interpretation (which is done by judges, not lawyers). If something is clearly criminal, don't do it. In the long term, part of the 'entrepreneurial chip' you will develop is legal judgement. This will tell you when to cut a corner and when a boundary must be respected.

Where do you find good 'professional' advice? I look for people who have just left a big partnership and are starting out on their own. They will be experienced, able and hungry for business. They will naturally understand your issues, as they are being entrepreneurial, too. You want the kind of relationship where you can call them up and chat for 5 to 10 minutes, and you will get their attention every time but not necessarily a bill.

By contrast, I find the most annoying lawyers or accountants to deal with are junior people in big companies, who have both big-company arrogance and junior-employee naïveté and caution.

So, as an entrepreneur, you should be building a 'consulting base' of:

1 Mentors, to help with inspiration and direction.

2 Experts from whom you get technical advice. Some of these will be 'professionals'.

At the same time, expand your knowledge base by reading relevant magazines (on- and offline) and above all good books, ones with depth and authorial voice rather than ones where a few ideas have been padded out to fill pages and where there is no discernible point of view. Talk to people. I think the current fad for 'networking' is overrated – I've been to a few 'networking' events, and they are just full of people trying to sell things. But it is good to socialise with other people in your business sector and learn as much as you can about what's happening and who's doing what.

Concept: The Hero's Journey

This is a useful notion for anyone setting off on, or even contemplating, a new venture. It works on two levels. First, the 'Journey' itself is a useful and often inspirational metaphor. Then there is an NLP change process based on it, which was created by Robert Dilts.

The Hero's Journey is based on the work of anthropologist and philosopher Joseph Campbell. Campbell analysed traditional stories from all round the world, and found that they followed a similar pattern (the research was then published in *The Hero with a Thousand Faces* in 1949). Since then, the book has been seized upon by Hollywood, who use it as a basic template for movie plots, but also by therapists seeking to give clients a metaphor for personal change and growth, especially in the face of a specific challenge. Here is a simplified version of the stages that Campbell unearthed.

The calling

The story begins with a hero (the term is used to describe protagonists of either sex). They are usually in a state that is in some way unsatisfactory, for them and for others around them. They receive a calling (in mythology, often via a 'herald' of some kind) to get up and do something about this state. This will mean going on a quest for a solution. Initially, they often refuse the call, as it involves too much risk or simply inconvenient change. Better to muddle along. However, things get worse and some event changes the hero's mind so they accept the call after all.

Entrepreneurs will recognise this sequence. It often manifests itself via an early feeling of discontent about some established way in which things are done, which is tolerated until a new, better way of doing them is understood. Or it can just be the slow, gathering awareness, from 'something ought to be done' to 'and I'm going to do it!' Entrepreneurs are familiar with that moment of 'accepting the call'. 'Yes, I'm going to give it a go.' (The sequence will repeat itself many times in the life of the business, every time a major decision looms.)

Confusion to clarity

Having decided to act, the hero has to leave their existing world and cross a threshold into a new one (for example, Alice falling down the rabbit hole). In this new world, they will experience confusion. However, a view of how things are will soon become clear:

the source of the trouble in the world they have left is a demon, and the demon is here in the new world and needs to be fought.

For the aspiring entrepreneur, the threshold is a metaphor for the 'dead weight of the past', old habits and expectations (like a salary cheque) and the voices, internal and external, telling you that this is all a waste of time and that if you went back to Megacorp and asked for your job back they'd say yes, and . . .

Confusion is a state familiar to all entrepreneurs, despite all our best attempts at planning. Resolve is needed here (and as an entrepreneur, you will have it).

The recognition of the demon is an important moment for any business. Some entrepreneurs find themselves on a cake-walk to wealth: that really is luck, and some people do have it. Most of us don't: there are blockages between us and success, and you won't really know what yours are until you get your business moving.

Gathering help

The hero knows they have to fight the demon – and that they haven't a hope of doing so on their own. They have to find help. Sometimes the help presents itself to them. The help can often be a wise old man or woman with magical powers. This person is a *mentor*. The mentor may provide some kind of magical protection (an amusing modern 'riff' on this is the array of gadgets given to 007 by Q about a third of the way through most Bond movies). Other *helpers* are gathered or attach themselves to the voyager (scarecrows, tin men and cowardly lions come to mind). With their mentor watching and their magic gizmo ready for use, the hero and his/her motley crew set off to do battle with the demon.

For the entrepreneur, the parallels are obvious. First, the realisation that, though in a profound sense this is your journey and your journey alone, you can't achieve your end without help.

Then, more specifically, the need for guidance from someone wise, someone with experience and perspective – a mentor. Sadly, there is no direct parallel for the magic protection: it can be seen as a metaphor for the mentor's wisdom, but I prefer to see it as a metaphor for your own energy, confidence and courage – things that have truly magical qualities. The helpers are the 'team' you assemble around you – other advisers and people who work for you.

The battle

The demon is finally confronted, fought and overcome. To make the story exciting, the good guys usually fare pretty badly at first. Then there is a turning point. Often at this moment the hero undergoes a transformation; they learn something of immense value or undergo some personal change that enables them to turn things around and win. Sometimes they have to make some kind of sacrifice to achieve victory (where the story is an initiation rite, the hero has to lose their youth and its privileges to be accepted into the adult world).

Often the demon turns out to be vulnerable and rather feeble once it has been rumbled. Sometimes it can even be co-opted as a helper for the hero – who, it must be remembered, has not come here just to biff demons but to solve a problem in the world they have left back there.

Victories in business are usually slower and more incremental than this dramatic showdown (though see the material later on 'Big Breaks'). However I like the part about the demon turning out to be both weaker than it appeared and a potential ally. Your competition may seem a demon – but can you learn from them, and are they helping build general awareness of your type of product? If your demon is fear of failure, remember that fear has a purpose too – to protect you. If fear makes you watch your cash more carefully or not break certain laws, it is helping you.

The return home

The hero often has to a steal from the demon some kind of magic 'elixir' that will right the wrongs of the world they left behind, then take that back to that world. In some stories, the hero will be reluctant to return: they have become triumphant in this new world and the old one doesn't really seem very alluring. In other stories, the hero, having stolen the elixir, is chased by supporters of the demon. In some of these, a posse from the old world has to come and rescue the hero. In the end, he or she returns with the elixir to the old world, delivers it, and gets on with life again, transformed – a hero, but still 'of the world'.

The elixir can be seen as your way of delivering value to your customers, that special thing that makes your enterprise something that they want to do business with. You probably did not have to escape hordes of vampire bats or warriors with ray-guns to bring it into being – but you've overcome many hurdles. It is precious, and you should be honoured for bringing it to the world.

The Hero's Journey

- Calling – rejected then accepted.
- Confusion to clarity.
- Gathering help – mentor plus 'motley crew'.
- The battle – impending defeat, transformation, victory.
- Return with the elixir.

Change Yourself: The Hero's Journey

Time to put this powerful tested metaphor to work for you, via this NLP technique.

First, you have to personalise the above story. What is your calling? What is the pain in the marketplace that you need to solve? What dead weight do you have to cast aside to take action? What creates confusion in your new, action-taking world? Who are your mentors? What is the demon you have to face? What transformation do you think you will have to undergo to defeat it? What is the elixir you intend to bring back to ease the pain of the old world where the story started?

I said 'who are your mentors?' (plural) and didn't mention helpers – two deviations from Campbell, who gave his hero one mentor plus a band of helpers. In this process, take as many mentors as you need (in practice, most people generally select around three) and ignore the concept of helpers. Select people you admire. It can be anyone: characters from literature, history, the movies, real life, people you know, people you love . . . These mentors should provide a range of qualities for you, such as strength, empathy, a sense of fun, wisdom (these are just examples – you know what you need). They must also 'deliver'. One time I asked a client who was extremely well-read to choose his three mentors, and he came up with Sartre, Kierkegaard and St Augustine. I sensed they'd been chosen at a purely intellectual level and would have little 'juice' in them, but we did the process anyway. Sure enough, the mentors didn't produce any noticeable shifts. In NLP we say 'no failure only feedback' – so we ran it again. This time he chose his dad, Nelson Mandela and a friend who was a very successful businessman. He said the difference was amazing.

The next stage is to undergo a mental enactment of the journey, using an NLP tool called a 'timeline'. Find a reasonably large room (a domestic sitting room is fine) and stand in the middle. Imagine a line laid out on the floor. Then imagine this line as representing a span of time, with the past at one end and the future at the other.

Now place the following *on* the timeline, in order:

1 **The present: where you are now.** As this is a forward-looking process, it helps to put this near the beginning of the line – in other words, to have much more future than past.

2 **The threshold.**

3 **The demon you will fight.** Leave quite a gap between the threshold and the demon, as you will be placing your mentors in this space.

4 **The elixir. Your goal.** What you will achieve at the end of this – the call answered and acted on successfully.

Next, place your mentors *beside*, not on, the timeline. 'Beside' means a pace or so off it, to the left or right, it doesn't matter which. As you have an imaginary line on the floor, it might help to have actual bits of paper showing where they are situated (people stumbling on a session of NLP work will often find pieces of paper on the floor, with participants standing on them or gazing fixedly at them).

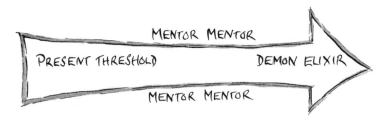

Crossing the threshold

Walk up to the threshold. Imagine you are faced by some physical impediment like a huge stone that has to be rolled away or a crevice you have to squeeze through. Then act out the rolling or squeezing. This may feel a bit odd, but do it anyway. (If you do this process with a friend acting as a 'coach', this person can help by telling you to push harder, or even acting as the impediment, physically pushing you back or holding on to you. You then need to work out a movement that will get you past – remember this is only a metaphor, so nothing too violent!) As you do this movement, think what actually constitutes the barrier. What is actually stopping you crossing into this new world?

The purpose of this action, which might seem odd to some people, is to help your unconscious mind communicate with you. Pushing at the threshold's pretend rock may bring to mind (to your *conscious* mind) what your misgivings about the new project really are. Sometimes we know these anyway; but other times we don't, and the realisation of exactly what we are pushing against can be illuminating. Sometimes our body communicates the necessary information to us when our thinking hasn't come up with the goods.

You might want to summon a mentor to help you remove the impediment. Push, push . . .

Pop! You're through, and in the confusing new world.

Meeting your mentors

Now walk up to the point on the timeline opposite where you placed your first mentor. Step onto the mentor's place, then turn and face an imaginary 'you' still on the line. Be the mentor addressing you. Go on, pretend to be them. Take on their posture and facial expression. Imagine wearing their clothes. Hear their voice. What are they saying? What are they offering you? (Imagine them actually handing some kind of gift to you.) As with pushing at the imaginary threshold, this is a way of letting your well-meaning but tongue-tied unconscious communicate with you. Let it. You may be very surprised by what emerges.

Once the mentor has spoken, step back onto the line, and be 'you' again. Turn to face the mentor and accept what they have said and/or given to you. If you want to have a dialogue with them, do so, remembering to step onto the space 'belonging' to the mentor when you want to speak as them, and to reoccupy your own space when you are speaking as you.

31

Then move up the line, to the point opposite where you have placed the next mentor.

Repeat the process for each one.

Claiming the elixir

At this point, the process deviates further from Campbell's story, in which you would now go and fight the demon. Walk straight past the demon, as if you had already won that battle, and stand on the point where the elixir is. You've won!

Turn to face back down the timeline. Ask yourself if there are any other resources you need to get across the threshold or to fight the demon.

(a) If the answer is *no* ... Imagine yourself sending all the gifts you have received on your journey (your mentors' words, any gifts they made to you) back to your original self, the 'you' that is still waiting to cross the threshold. Make a gesture as you do so.

(b) If the answer is *'yes*, I still need x' ... If what you need is material (e.g. £10,000), just imagine for the moment that you have that. If the answer is another personal quality, imagine a mentor who will bestow that quality on you, then go back to the 'meeting your mentors' section of the process and meet this new mentor. Then walk past the demon again, and ask again if you still need further resources. No? Take option (a). Yes? Rerun option (b).

Then walk back beside, not on the timeline, which has 'magical powers', and not treading on any of your mentors, to your original starting point. Face back up the line and accept the gifts that you sent back from the point of the elixir.

Finale

Now, armed with these gifts, make your way back up the line. Push past the threshold again. Pause, maybe, by each mentor and acknowledge them. When you get to the demon, you probably won't have to fight it. Instead, notice how it has altered. Most people I take through this process notice a remarkable change in the demon. It has become a shadow of its former self. It may be a kind of husk or ruin that you can step over without much thought. Or it may even want to offer you something helpful. Move the demon off the line – give it a 'place' like a mentor – then step into that place and give yourself advice from the demon's perspective. I did this with a client whose demon was her business partner; when she did this part of the process, she realised that her partner had her best interests at heart. Afterwards, she told me that that was the point in the process where she had got the most benefit.

Walk to the elixir again, and pause a while there, reminding yourself of all the gifts you possess.

Finally, walk back (off the line) to the start, and walk slowly up the line to the elixir again. Pause, then walk back off the line to the start. Walk slowly up the line again. Do this a few times, until you are satisfied that the process has delivered to you all the benefit it can.

There, that's it. People unfamiliar with NLP (or therapy generally) might find all this walking up and down 'timelines' and pretending to be Nelson Mandela (or whoever) a bit odd. I suppose it *is* a bit odd, but it works. I have done this process with many people from many walks of life, some of them pretty hard-bitten, no-nonsense types, and it invariably produces significant changes in attitude and awareness. Actually, it is often with the hard-bitten, no-nonsense types that it works best. These people have got out of the habit of trying to communicate with their unconscious, but this does not mean that their unconscious is not still trying to communicate with them, and this process gives it a chance.

For example … Keith was a relatively new entrepreneur, who wanted his business to become a market leader. He identified his demon as a fear of going after new business. He chose three mentors – two friends who were successful entrepreneurs and the explorer Sir Wilfred Thesiger. From the two entrepreneurs he gleaned self-confidence and determination, and from Sir Wilfred the belief that apparently 'impossible' things can be done. Each time he was 'addressed' by the mentors he felt a real change in his mental state, and by the time he walked past the demon he realised it was beaten already. In fact, he saw that the demon was trying to protect him, and took from it a quality of concern for others, which would make his drive for new business less about 'selling' and more about providing customers with what they needed.

People more aware of therapeutic practice will notice the strong influence of Fritz Perls, his 'Gestalt' therapy in general and the 'empty chair' technique in particular.

Getting started

Do a deal as quickly as possible
- Five-minute business plan.
- Be positive about selling.

Learn the entrepreneurial way
- Doing business is the best teacher.

Build a consulting base
- You may do it by yourself, but you don't have to do it on your own.
- Mentors.
- Tips.
- Professional advisors.

Concept: The Hero's Journey ...
... is your journey.

02

A solid platform

Do you have a business or just a clever idea? In the early life of an enterprise it's not always easy to tell. A few contacts may buy and like what you've provided, but can you spread the net wider, and start attracting a substantial customer base? Can you do so profitably and repeatably?

In this chapter, I am assuming this threshold has been crossed. I shall look at the key issues that arise at this moment. To run a business successfully requires a wide range of skills. Nobody possesses the full complement 'naturally'; some of these will have to be learnt. To assist this, I have broken this range down into four 'Capability Sets'. Resources also have to be gathered – I look at the most important ones that you will need. In the 'Concept' section of the chapter I shall present some NLP tools that come in particularly handy at this time in the business' life, and in the 'Change Yourself' section, an exercise based on the four Capability Sets and one of the NLP tools to help develop that all-important 'entrepreneurial chip'.

The moment you know 'there really is a business in this!' is a great one – but also a kind of expulsion from a garden of innocence: the going gets tougher from here on. You will be devoting more time to the business. You will have to start selling to people who don't really know you. (Some businesses avoid this problem, but most don't.) Most pressing of all, you will have to start running the business like a business.

When you start up, you should deliver as well as you can, but behind it there will probably be a lot of improvising. Most entrepreneurs find this rather fun, but sadly, the party has to end. The whole thing has to become much more systematic. This means buckling down and doing stuff you don't like. ('But I started my own business so that I wouldn't have to do things I don't like!' Bad luck.) This means two things: repetitive tasks and tasks you're not particularly good at. And sometimes, tasks that are both!

The repetitive stuff first ... There's a lot of material around today on how starting a business is an adventure. It's all about your flair, your pazzazz, your creativity – forget sailing round the world, falling in love or climbing Mount Everest; enterprise is the romantic challenge of the twenty-first century! I agree – but at the same time, people embarking on the Starship Enterprise need to understand that a lot of it is about doing simple, repetitive, unromantic things as well.

I'm talking about basic admin: things like writing and sending letters and emails; about making sales calls and invoicing (and chasing the invoices when the customer doesn't pay up. And chasing them again when the customer still doesn't pay up ...) Companies House and HMRC will require forms to be filled in. Computers may go wrong: if you can't fix them yourself, 'an expert' has to be called in. And so on – as every person who has started a business knows.

People who come to entrepreneurship straight from school or the street aren't aware of how much of this stuff there is. (Hint – get an office job for six months, just to find out.) People who come from smart careers in consultancies may have once been aware but have usually forgotten, as other people did all the grunt work for them. (If you have to go into town to get a new set of letterheads printed, it may take an hour and a half. 'But I used to charge £125 an hour for my work!' the consultant-turned-entrepreneur moans. Congratulations; you've just rejoined the human race.)

Of course, in time, when the business is up and running, you will be able to appoint a PA. More on that later: right now you can't afford such a luxury. Part of my pride in being an entrepreneur is in my ability to get my head down and do this dull stuff in a solid reliable manner.

The second way in which entrepreneurship is unromantic is broader. Many entrepreneurs have a skill around which they build their business. This is what they like doing and they do it well. But unless they back up what is essentially a 'delivery' skill with a portfolio of essential business skills, they will not turn it into a business. It's a rather boring analogy, but an enterprise can be seen as one of those forms with a set of boxes, all of which you have to tick. It doesn't matter how brilliant you are at ticking one of them; if you leave one box, or several, unticked, your business will probably not make it.

The Beermat Entrepreneur, one of my favourite business books, talks about getting 'cornerstones', experts in key business skills, to tick these boxes for you. This is something you need to do – later. You can't afford to hire these people straight away, and actually it is best to do all the stuff yourself to start with. When you start hiring people, you will need to assign jobs to them and have them report to you. Unless you have a pretty good understanding of what the jobs involve, you will not be able to assign tasks correctly or assess how they have been carried out. You have to know how to do things before you can manage anyone else doing them.

A small business is not a collective, it is essentially a one-person show. You are in charge, which means that you must at first do, then manage all the aspects of your business. When I hear an entrepreneur say, 'I let Tricia worry about the finance; she's good at that sort of stuff', I worry. US President Harry S. Truman had a sign on his desk which read 'The buck stops here.'

The four Capability Sets

So what sets of skills do you need to master? The answer is 'loads'. There are numerous ways of classifying them; I like to break them down into four groups. I've called them 'Capability Sets' rather than just 'skill sets' to fit them into a model which I shall introduce in the next chapter.

Few people go into business fully armed with all the skills – most new entrepreneurs are good at some, appalling at others and adequate at the rest. The right reaction to this is to fill the 'holes' by reading all you can on the subject, by finding an expert and firing questions at them, by attending formal courses of study, and, of course, by learning from the entrepreneur's principal tutor – trial and error. Sadly, a common reaction is to ignore the holes, thinking 'they don't really matter' or 'it'll be fine'. Such a reaction greatly increases the chances of business failure.

Capabilities do not require personality change: they can be mastered, and are regularly mastered by people of all ages who go into business.

Capability Set 1: Leadership

This covers a range of skills. The ability to *motivate and manage people* is a key one – especially the ability to motivate and manage yourself. Entrepreneurs are self-starters and get things done. The ability to *innovate* is another: not so much great technical innovation as mental agility and improvisatory skills. Entrepreneurs get things done imaginatively and quickly. There are also the skills of *strategy* and *decision making*, and I would like to discuss these two here.

By 'strategy', I mean the ability to develop a vision of where you are headed, and, behind that, visions of both how you will get there and why you deserve to.

The vision is 'where I want the business to be in x years' time' (5 is a good number for x, but try it with x equalling several numbers). The hows and whys of strategy are about your business model. Two key questions:

1 What value do I offer my customers?

2 How do I make money out of what I do?

The first is a *marketing* strategy question – the answer is what marketers call your 'USP' (Unique Selling Point), the special reason why customers come to you rather than to someone else. The second is about your 'business model'. It is finance-related, but is a question for an entrepreneur, not a pure finance person.

Some people naturally answer these questions imaginatively and effectively; others get to do so by study and practice. Look at markets; think 'how could things be done differently?' Look at businesses and think where they make their money (the answer is not always obvious).

The 'business imagination' you develop will come in handy over and over again, not just as you design new products or even businesses, but as you solve the endless problems that crop up as you run your existing business.

Decision making is largely a matter of developing your 'entrepreneurial chip'. I believe that anyone can develop such a chip, even someone not naturally decisive.

Capability Set 2: Administration and operations

These are the 'getting stuff done' capabilities.

By *administration*, I mean understanding the basics of office management and, later, things like payroll. I also mean the basics of project management: how to break a project down into various tasks; how to set these tasks out in the order in which they need to be done (sometimes sequential, other times overlapping); how to make sure you have the resources you need in place before each task; how you will know when a task is complete.

Operations covers what you have to do to create and deliver the product or service, repeatedly, reliably and profitably. It is about 'delivery', but also about managing that delivery.

I believe operations to be the most important part of business. However good an idea you have – if you can't do this stuff, you do not have a business. Sorry to be unromantic, but a lot of business is about having and operating a 'sausage machine'.

However, it's actually not as uncreative as it sounds. Most people in corporate jobs are simply operating a tiny part of a much bigger machine. You get to design, build and continuously improve the machine. These are creative activities.

Successful entrepreneurs develop what I call an 'operational vision'. This is not their big, overall vision of their product and how it is going to change the markets it sells into, but a lower-level vision of how their business actually works. It's about designing, implementing and improving the systems and processes which make the right things happen at the right times in a cost-effective way. This is a challenging activity. It is also a slow activity; a marathon, not a sprint. It involves learning by doing (and getting wrong) and so takes time. My view is that it takes a couple of years to get these right – early experiments fail; you start getting it right; you hone and improve.

Learning by doing is not easy: as my coach said to me, an entrepreneur 'learns to fly the plane while they are still building it'. Personally I'd rather fly in a complete plane with a qualified pilot, but as an entrepreneur, you don't have that luxury. Instead, enjoy the challenge, and respect your achievements at it.

The Japanese, by and large self-effacing people, conquered the business world in the 1970s and 1980s by quietly mastering operations. They worked at their processes, following the principle of *kaizen*, which means continuous improvement.

I shall talk more about time management (the key to great ops) and about systems thinking (the key to great ops strategy) later.

Finally, for some businesses, for example those in the technology sector, operations require a high level of *technical expertise*. Most businesses don't need this, however: most of the entrepreneurs I know are not experts at any kind of technology, just astute business people who know when to hire the right technical people. If you have great expertise in some technology, that's great, but you still have to build a business around it with customers, finance, suppliers, processes, a team (and so on).

Capability Set 3: Finance and legal

These are essentially protective capabilities.

By *finance*, I mean anything to do with money, not just the raising of capital. It's a topic where a lot of people I coach have a serious blind spot. They have decided that they are useless at it, and that's that. Often this comes from having some kind of trauma with learning maths as a child – a bullying teacher or an exasperated parent. As adult entrepreneurs, this is irrational. It is also irrelevant: you don't need to be good at maths to do basic finance. Can you enter figures into an Excel spreadsheet? That's all the maths you need. OK, you can't work out the 10-year discounted cash flow from a currency swap bond derivative. Neither can I. Start-up finance is to mathematics what the Teletubbies Annual is to literary studies.

A nice quote from Alan Sugar: 'I thought PE was something you did in the gym till I was earning a million a year.' (For non-finance people, PE is the price/earnings ratio, a way of valuing shares.)

You will need to know basic 'money-watching' techniques such as double-entry bookkeeping, simple profit and loss accounts, balance sheets and cash-flow management.

You must acquire a feel for the monetary basics of your business. What are the main sources of cost, and how much do they set you back a month? How much product do you need to sell, firstly to cover these costs, then to make a decent profit?

Learn to get restless at the thought of assets sitting around idle: they are actually wasting you money. Develop a streak of meanness: accountants in big companies spend a lot of time telling everyone else in the business that they can't spend money on x, y and z – now that's your job. Above all, think cash. Cash, not profit, is king.

Of course, raising capital is important. I shall discuss this in more detail later in the chapter.

The good news about finance is that the basic skills can easily be learnt. There are loads of courses. Chris has co-authored a book aimed at entrepreneurs called *Finance on a Beermat*, which contains all the information you need (even if it does urge you to get a 'cornerstone' much sooner than I would).

I bracket *law* with finance, as both are essentially about rules that you transgress at your peril. For most businesses, finance is an ever-present issue while law (hopefully) only raises its head occasionally. On those occasions it can be of extreme importance. You need to know the basics of company law and, most important, the law around your particular business. Have a lawyer who really understands your sector.

Capability Set 4: Sales, making 'friends' and marketing

Guy Kawasaki says:

'Forget "I think therefore I am". For entrepreneurs the salient phrase is "I pitch therefore I am". Pitching isn't only useful for raising money – it's an essential tool for reaching agreement on any subject: management buy-in for developing a product or service, closing a sale, securing a partnership, recruiting an employee, or securing an investment.'

The *sales* role is often associated with mavericks and charmers, and many people in the sales profession seem to buy into this stereotype. Entrepreneurs can be dazzled by this, and think that in order to sell, they must hire a smooth-talking guy who drives a Porsche. However, most sales work is about process – getting lists of prospects, qualifying them, setting up sales visits, following up. And the key to this is application and method: in other words, it's more solid boring stuff.

The most successful salespeople are often not charismatic. They are quiet but determined, and follow correct procedures. They establish 'rapport' (more on this below); they listen; they explain clearly why their product or service matches the needs of that customer.

Certain sales skills, such as handling objections and closing, need to be learnt, as must the psychological skill of handling rejection. But these can be learnt, and are just another part of the toolkit that an entrepreneur must master. As with finance, there are loads of courses and books.

Sales skills can be transferred to the more general task of *making friends for the business*. People often think of businesses as a delivery machine plus customers. While this is true up to a point, the reality is much more complex. A business needs a wider circle of relationships. Your mentor, for example, who will go out of their way to provide advice and referrals.

Wise entrepreneurs build good relationships with their suppliers. Arguably these are more important than individual customers. If a customer disappears, you can find others; if a supplier suddenly lets you down, you can be in big trouble (I've seen businesses fail because of this). A good deal from a supplier can provide a huge boost. Felix Dennis, the publisher, effectively started his business career with such a break: a printer agreed to print his first magazine without money upfront, based on a promise from some retailers. Many magazines and millions of pounds later, Dennis still uses the same printer.

This general, 'friend-making' skill is very important. Some people have it naturally. For others, there are courses on things like influencing skills. Dale Carnegie courses are still running, after almost 100 years (so they must be doing something right). And, of course, you can study NLP.

I learnt many of these skills from my mother. She is a very charming individual who has a great capacity to engage people in her endeavours, no matter how minor. I remember her persuading a ticket agent to get front-row tickets for Evita. She told him the whole story of why the tickets were so important – it was a present for close relatives' 25th wedding anniversary; they lived in the country and rarely got to see shows (etc.). She managed to engage the agent to such a degree that he became emotionally involved with her project and rang around all the other agents until he came up with the tickets.

By *marketing*, I do not mean expensive market research programmes, promotional campaigns or big 'PR pushes', which are beyond the scope of most start-up businesses. What I mean is the acquisition of market knowledge.

Successful entrepreneurs come to understand their market like the back of their hand. How things are done; what's changing and how; what sort of customers buy what sort of products and why; who the 'movers and shakers' are. This knowledge runs much deeper than figures about market sizes and growth rates. Entrepreneurs are forever on the lookout for more to know about their sector – a friend of mine who runs a large training business likens it to teenagers and fashion. They are hungry for knowledge; they keep their eyes and ears open; they learn from mistakes. As with mastering the structural aspects of your business, I reckon it takes two years to become truly market savvy – savvy about your market, not 'markets' in some general sense.

Leaping with both feet into a sector where you lack market knowledge can lead to unpleasant results. I know one entrepreneur who had all the other skills, piled into a sector he didn't understand, and managed to lose £1m. (Yes, other entrepreneurs such as Richard Branson specialise in charging into sectors and shaking them up. But they have teams of advisors and mountains of cash.)

I'm not saying 'stick to what you know'; I am saying 'to succeed, you must become a market expert'. If you know nothing now, start learning fast. There are unlikely to be courses on this kind of knowledge – though there might be. For example, if you are learning a skill such as design at college, there may be a module on the business aspects. Take this module! Otherwise your learning will have to be 'on the hoof'. Get learning fast.

As I have said, the entrepreneur needs an above-average competence at all of the above. Ignoring any of them will cause problems. Often entrepreneurs are good at one, passable at another, worry about and work on a third, and ignore a fourth – which turns out to be the one that 'blows up in their face'.

Gathering other resources

Now the business is serious, it will need other resources, too. First among these is . . .

Money

Raising money is a combination of making financial sense and skilful pitching. Find out what numbers the financers want to see and deliver it in that format. In the past I have gone into banks with a blank sheet of paper, asked them 'what do you need to know?', presented the relevant information from memory – and got the loan.

Of course, the best way to finance your business is from cash flow: having enough money coming in so you don't need any outside finance. Jam today as well as jam tomorrow. If this is not possible, do some kind of deal that earns you some money, then start your business. Any kind of wheeze will do – buy something cheap and sell it on to someone else for more. (You may find you have a knack for this, and that in the end this will be your business.)

At some point, you will probably need to borrow from the bank. Finding the right bank can be difficult. As with any major decision, get all the information you can first. This information will be about people, not products. Most bank products are depressingly the same; the difference that makes the difference is the individual manager. Ask local business people whom they like and respect. (Ask for a referral to that person if an obvious candidate emerges, though if you don't, you can just call them up: banks want your business.) Arrange to meet some other bank managers, too. Whom did you 'click' with best? Personal chemistry is what matters most here.

When you get a manager, they may suddenly get moved by the bank. If you can, move with them. If you can't, unless you really like the replacement, you will have to start looking all over again. Banks don't let you pick and choose managers. So pick and choose banks. A number of entrepreneurs I know have two banks to guard against the sudden removal of a liked and trusted manager.

I have never used angel investors. The property business was naturally suited to debt funding (nice assets to borrow against); the others (few assets but healthy revenue streams) have self-funded, with a bit of help from the bank at times. I accept that other businesses may have different requirements, but often see investor relationships going wrong, so advise against this route if at all possible.

Two classic scenarios:

1 Someone invests because they like you; it goes wrong; blame starts flying around; the money, the friendship and the business end up down the drain.

2 The investor is ruthless; things start going wrong; they step in to protect their investment and you are no longer in control of your business.

Both of these happen regularly, and neither is desirable.

It's important to understand that the moment you cede even a small stake in your business to an outsider, your level of control and freedom sinks markedly, as you have an obligation to that person.

If you must get investors in, make sure you make a realistic assessment of how much money you need. Pitch too low, and you will end up having to ask for more money and giving away more of your business. Pitch too high and you will not be taken seriously. It's better to make a mistake in the latter direction than the former: you can always negotiate down.

How much equity should you give away? My father had a motto, 'half the show for all the dough'. But better still, keep all the show and all the dough yourself.

Technical expertise

Just to reiterate the point: this on its own doesn't make a business. However, most businesses will need some of this. For some, it is provided by a specific cornerstone, a boffin who is at the heart of the team. For many others, however, it is not. It's amazing how quickly a focused, determined entrepreneur can become an expert at what they need to know.

When I went into property I knew nothing about property law. I asked a solicitor what the relevant acts were, then went out and bought them. I read them and noted the parts that seemed to have meaning for my business. Another chat with the solicitor confirmed I was correct. From then on, each time a major law came through (every three or four years), I repeated this process. It took very little time, no more time than reading a long novel. I found it turned me into an 'expert', outperforming highly qualified solicitors who had broad knowledge but did not really understand the subtleties of the very 'niche' area in which I had built my business. I am now able to teach this knowledge to young people in my business, who don't all have university degrees but are smart, and who can now carry on the mantle of outperforming the so-called experts.

Allies

I've already talked about this, but will restate it here: your business needs friends. Not just customers, though they are hugely important, but suppliers and mentors. I have found that once solicitors, accountants (even auditors) and other professionals get to know you and get emotionally involved in the business, they will take you under their wing. In times of change or trouble, having good advisors on board is invaluable.

Premises

Most start-ups don't need to worry about these. I started my first businesses from home and didn't rent an office until one of the businesses was earning more than £150,000 p.a. With the internet and advanced telephone systems, you can give the impression of having a large business, without incurring significant costs. When you start out, some nice stationery, a reasonable website and a telephone answering service is all you need to send out the right message of professionalism. Many entrepreneurs start even simpler, with just a mobile phone number.

Quitting your job

If you are a natural entrepreneur and you are currently in employment, you may want to quit your job at this time. But remember that it can take two years to master a business. You are still way short of that. How will you survive in those two years? Many people make the move from employee to entrepreneur gradually, by becoming a contractor (often back in the same company). This is a wise step, though make sure you don't drift back into being a full-time worker for them, now minus pension and other rights. Aim to have at least two working days a week focusing on your business.

My dad used to say, 'Always expect something from left-field.' Business has a habit of throwing things at you when you least expect them. Give yourself a little bit of extra money or time to provide for the unexpected.

Concepts: Rapport, congruence and anchoring

In a business that is 'up and running', these NLP techniques prove extremely helpful. They are all based on one of the underlying principles of NLP, of what I call 'physical intelligence'. Research into physiology is showing that areas like the heart and the intestines have more neurology than is simply needed to monitor and control them. Do these organs have some kind of intelligence? It might sound odd, but consider the following:

- Our language is full of metaphors that imply exactly such a thing. 'My heart wasn't in it.'

- Sports practice is essentially about physical learning. When Chris took up golf recently, his coach told him that 'You'll become good at this shot when your whole body has learnt it.' (In this case, the learning is proving rather slow…)

- We are all familiar with the experience of 'gut feel', where we know something to be the case, even if our conscious, rational mind denies it.

It seems that we can at least learn and store information all over our bodies, and maybe in the case of gut feel, make subconscious assessments of situations. NLP teaches us to use this untapped capability.

Rapport

This is most obviously useful in a sales situation, or any other kind of pitch where you are aiming to convince someone of your business' worth.

Observe a great one-to-one communicator at work, someone who is known for their charm and ease of manner. They will often adjust their voice-tone, speech-rhythm and vocabulary to match that of the person to whom they are talking – we talk about 'speaking to someone in their language'. But they will also 'speak to the person in their *body* language', adopting a similar body posture and using similar gestures. Yet at the same time, this does not come across as forced or as mimicry. It is a natural dropping-into-step with a fellow human being, a way of signalling that they, the communicator, are sympathetic. It shows that, although they may have different views or a different agenda, they are at a deeper level 'on the same wavelength'. The person on the receiving end of this will feel relaxed and valued.

NLP calls this process *mirroring*, and this end product *rapport*.

People who are natural salespeople are often innately good at establishing rapport. The rest of us have to learn how to do this, and this learning can be tricky – the moment you start mirroring consciously it looks forced and can appear rude. The best hint I know for avoiding this is to stop trying to mirror. Instead, just observe the other person. Not in any interpretative way (they're doing x, so they must be feeling y) but just purely noticing things like:

■ their voice-tone and pitch

■ their 'pace' – are they breathing fast or slow, speaking fast or slow?

■ their posture

■ any repeated gestures

■ their facial expression.

This is respectful, not intrusive. As you do this, you will find yourself naturally drifting into mirroring patterns of gesture or speech.

Note that it doesn't matter what you are actually talking about. This is about what NLP calls 'process', what's going on, not 'content', what is actually being said.

Anyone dubious about the above should watch poor communicators at work. A pushy salesman leans forward to an already defensive prospect and raises his voice. A nervous teenager avoids all eye contact and starts fiddling with her lapel.

The skills you use to mirror and establishing rapport can also be put to use passively, to enhance your skill at reading people and situations.

Jane, a salesperson from a large company, left to set up her own business selling a training product to the insurance industry. She told me that she had a set procedure for selling to companies. When asked to present, she would go with another salesperson. The salesperson would do the actual presentation: Jane would sit and just watch the body language of the prospects around the table. She said that within two or three minutes she could identify how the decision-making process worked in that company. She could tell from gestures, nods and facial expressions who made the decision, who was required to support that decision, who could influence that decision, and who had no bearing on that decision.

Her business grew to a turnover of £20,000,000 in two and a half years.

Congruence

This is very useful in decision making.

When coaching people, I often hear them say things like 'I am going to change all those bad habits right now.' Powerful stuff – if they really mean it. The best way to tell if they really mean it is to check their body language. Are they sitting up, leaning forward, bright-eyed, animated? Or still hunched in their seat? If the latter is the case, that usually means the client is expressing a wish rather than an intention. (One has to learn to interpret each individual's set of gestures – everybody speaks a slightly different body language.) If someone makes a statement that is backed up by the right body language, NLP says that the person is *congruent* (the usage has slipped a bit; now we also talk about the statement being congruent).

You can monitor your own physical reactions to statements and, most useful of all, decisions. We have all had the experience of agreeing to something, yet at the same time feeling uneasy about it. Such an agreement is not congruent. I find that monitoring my decision making for congruence very helpful. If there is incongruence, it's time to step back and ask what my subconscious is trying to tell me. As incongruence is often felt as a physical sensation somewhere in the body, I actually imagine myself asking that sensation what it is trying to tell me, and just noticing what comes into my mind. It sounds odd, but it often comes up with really useful information. When it doesn't work, a more rational approach is needed – go over the pros and cons of the decision again.

Over time, you will become better at attending to your feelings, at listening to the 'voice' of your physical intelligence at work. One important distinction to make is between the 'gut instinct' message of incongruence and internal feelings of fear. The former means 'back off'. The latter means that the new, correct decision will catapult you into a new situation or challenge, which is naturally a bit scary. Deal with the fear.

Anchoring

I use this technique as a coach, to prepare entrepreneurs for important meetings. It uses the learning aspect of physical intelligence, more specifically learning by association. We are very good at this: think how a specific piece of music can catapult you back to happy (or sad) memories of people, places, times. . .

Try this exercise:

1 Think hard about a time when you were really confident.

2 You may find yourself scanning your memory for a few moments, then your subconscious will come up with something. You will probably break out into a great big smile at that point.

3 As soon as you know you have found an appropriately confident memory, and while the memory is at the forefront of your mind, pinch yourself (gently). Anywhere will do; the fleshy lower section of a forefinger is a good spot, but it's your choice.

4 'Break state' – move, shake your head, move your mind and body on from that memory.

5 Pinch yourself in the same place.

Does the memory – and with it, the feeling of confidence – come back? If not, repeat the exercise. Make sure that you carry out step 3 when the memory is not only present but at its most powerful.

When stage 5 makes the memory comes back, you have carried out the NLP process called anchoring. (The pinch is anchor; when you first do it, in step 3, that is called 'applying' the anchor; step 5, when you pinch yourself to bring back the state, is called 'firing' the anchor.) Do this exercise to prepare for potentially stressful situations.

Anchors can also take other forms.

Gestures

People who have little rituals before they carry out a difficult action are often mocked, but they are anchoring a state of readiness. I recommend developing rituals like this, as long as they are not too public and don't invite negative comments from other people, which will defeat their object of getting you into a good state. (Even in public, some people 'anchor'. Peter Schmeichel gave both goalposts a tap with his boot before every game, in front of 60,000 people at Old Trafford, and rugby fans will be aware of Johnny Wilkinson's pre-kick rituals – a classic piece of anchoring.)

Places

('Spatial anchoring'.) Remember the Hero's Journey process, where certain parts of the floor became associated with a threshold, with mentors, with a demon and with an elixir? This was essentially anchoring, creating an association between a piece of physical space and a set of ideas, feelings and gestures.

An image

Some people prefer to imagine some kind of image or symbol and associate the positive feeling to that image. When they bring the image to mind, the feeling comes back.

Sound

The Beatles' *All You Need Is Love* works brilliantly for me. It takes me straight back to a time when I did work on the Logical Levels in Santa Cruz, and brings a fantastic feeling of purpose, clarity, wonder and happiness.

Finally, note that anchors can also be negative. Are there things in your workplace with negative associations? Get rid of them.

Change Yourself: The I-D-EA-S process

"Vision without action is a daydream; action without vision is a nightmare."

Japanese proverb

Large companies are run by boards, where a group of people with complementary skills are gathered together. Options will be viewed from different perspectives before decisions are made. Working alone, the entrepreneur has to create those perspectives for him- or herself. This process is a way of establishing those perspectives, using anchoring and a refinement of the four Capability Sets.

When confronted by a problem, you anchor four perspectives, and access them one by one. You let each 'have its say' without interruptions from the others. Once each has fully expressed itself, you have aligned the combined wisdom of these sometimes competing but necessary viewpoints: what follows is usually good, robust and well thought-out decision.

INNOVATOR DOER EXTERNAL STAKEHOLDER
ADVISOR

1 The first mindset you need to access is that of an Innovator (part of the Leadership capability). Think of a time when anything seemed possible and you were being creative. It does not need to be a significant event, you could be dreaming up going on an adventurous holiday. Enjoy this feeling of possibility, imagination, creativity... When you have a strong sense of being imaginative and creative, press the knuckle on your *index* finger until the feeling starts to fade. Pause for a short while and then press the knuckle again; you should find that the feeling returns. If not, repeat

a few times until it does. You have now anchored this state of mind.

a few times until it does. You have now anchored this state of mind.

a few times until it does. You have now anchored this state of mind.

2 Next, anchor the 'operations' capability, the Doer. Think of a time when you were either getting on with something, or making a clear, rigorous plan of how you were going to get on and do something. Enjoy the buzz of activity. When you have a strong sense of this, press the knuckle on your *middle* finger until the feeling starts to fade. Pause for a short while and then press the knuckle again; you should find that the feeling returns. If not, repeat a few times until it does. You have now anchored this state of mind.

3 Next, anchor the 'protective' role of an External Advisor such as an accountant or lawyer. I find it best to see this person as both critical and caring, like a rather traditional type of parent. Their role is to look at options and consider what might go wrong. At the same time, they are not just criticising for the hell of it – they are there to spot dangers and advise against rash courses of action. Think of a time when you realised things were suddenly getting out of control and you seized back that control, stopping activity and subjecting your current position to rigorous analysis. When you have a strong sense of being analytical, aware of danger and in control, press the knuckle on your *ring* finger until the feeling starts to fade. (As above) pause for a short while and then press the knuckle again; you should find that the feeling returns. If not, repeat a few times until it does. You have now anchored this state of mind.

4 Finally anchor the perspective that focuses on the world out there, the world of stakeholders in the company – customers, markets, the public in general. The state you want to access here is one of empathy. Think of a time when you were really attuned to someone else; you knew how they thought and felt, without knowing how you knew this (and they let you know that you were right – this wasn't just

mind-reading plus wishful thinking). When you have a strong sense of this, press the knuckle on your *little* finger until the feeling starts to fade. Pause for a short while and then press the knuckle again; you should find that the feeling returns. If not, repeat a few times until it does. You have now anchored this state of mind.

5 Now bring to mind the project you are thinking about.

6 Press the Innovator knuckle and brainstorm lots of ideas. Be very optimistic and create an ideal scenario for a year or two's time.

7 Press the Doer knuckle and put together a practical plan to get to that scenario. Be specific – what's the first step, the second, the third…? The Doer is also a planner, and very good at this kind of meticulous work.

8 Press the External Advisor knuckle and ask yourself: what could go wrong? You should end up with a set of criticisms of the plan.

9 Press the Stakeholder knuckle and consider how the action will impact on other people such as a typical customer, a key supplier, your capital providers (if you have any) and even a family member. You may notice conflicts between people who want you to follow your planned course of action and those who don't.

10 Return to the Innovator and come up with solutions to the issues raised by the External Advisors concerning the Doer's plan. Balance the needs of people 'out there' who are resistant to the plan and those who want to be involved.

11 Spend time not touching any knuckle; this is when you are using another part of the leadership capability, that of the decision maker.

12 Repeat as necessary.

A solid platform

Know when you have an idea worth going for

Develop a competence for each of the four Capability Sets:

■ *Leadership* – innovation, motivation, strategic thinking, decisiveness.

■ *Operations and admin* – getting things done, keeping things working.

■ *Finance and legal* – protection.

■ *Sales, making friends and marketing* – interacting with the world out there.

Gather the resources you need

Concepts: rapport, congruence and anchoring

I-D-EA-S

■ A process to simulate a team of advisors helping you with a decision.

■ Over time, will build into your entrepreneurial chip.

03

Aligning your mind for success

In this chapter I shall look in depth at certain beliefs and values concerning risk, decisions, luck and conventional morality, that seem to mark out us entrepreneurs from the rest of the world. Then I shall put these beliefs and values into the bigger context of an overall model of human psychology called the Logical Levels.

The Logical Levels is one of the most powerful tools to have emerged from NLP. The word 'holistic' is grossly overused in both psychology and management, but the Levels model truly deserves to be called this. It is a synthesis of many models of thinking and motivation (and demotivation!).

Finally I shall put this model to use in a specifically entrepreneurial context, via a process I have developed called the Seven Parallels. This may sound a bit mystical, but there's no need to get out the joss-sticks – this is practical piece of change work, that examines your own motivational levels, the needs of your business, and the fit (or lack of fit) between the two.

Entrepreneurial beliefs and values

To start, let's look at some core entrepreneurial beliefs and values that help us act independently and effectively. Beliefs and values about . . .

Risk

To both the classical economic theorist and the person in the street, entrepreneurs are people who take risks. There is a measure of truth in this, but it's wrong to over-glamorise this belief.

Entrepreneurs take *calculated* risks, not just risks. Two teenagers playing 'chicken' by driving cars at each other are taking risks. Entrepreneurs don't do this. They may take one big risk, in backing both themselves and their business imagination against all those voices telling them to 'play safe'. However, after that, they spend a lot of time and energy minimising risk on a day-to-day basis.

'Entrepreneurs don't just throw themselves off cliffs and start flapping,' says Paul, a friend who runs his own energy business. He adds with a grin, 'We might try abseiling, however . . .'

Entrepreneurs understand – and don't see why other people don't understand – that there are risks in *not* being entrepreneurial, too. There is no guaranteed job-for-life in the modern marketplace. Even the most successful corporate managers can find themselves victims of a take-over, after which the function they have managed so brilliantly gets moved to Western China and they are given the choice of relocating to the fringes of the Taklamakan Desert or the sack.

Outside certain civil service or local government posts, there is no guaranteed security. There is, though, a real and present threat that having given up on your dreams at 20 to join a big safe organisation, at 45 you will be jettisoned by that organisation – without the survival skills that 25 years of entrepreneurship would have given you.

'Maybe,' doubters reply, 'but surely even the sack at 45 is better than business failure and bankruptcy, which can be the fate of the unwary entrepreneur?' I would make two ripostes to this. First, there is a whole range of enterprise outcomes, of which spectacular crashing and burning is only one, at the far end of a long and varied continuum. Most businesses that 'fail' simply run out of steam: they bump along the bottom for a bit, making some money but not enough, until the entrepreneur finds something more challenging and potentially rewarding. (Similarly, most 'successful' businesses grow quietly and unspectacularly, yielding a stream of benefits for their owners, staff and customers but never making it to the 'Tycoon of the Month' profiles in the business press.)

Second, even bankruptcy is not the end of the line for the true entrepreneur. I don't want to go down the happy-clappy route of saying bankruptcy is just a tumble off your horse. If you have substantial assets tied up in the business, it can be a terrible thing (so do all you can to avoid it: do you really need that loan your smiling bank manager is offering in return for a charge on your house?) Even if you don't lose personal assets, others will suffer: people to whom you owe money, many of whom will be entrepreneurs like yourself. But in the end, the collapse of a business must be viewed as a regrettable event, not a terminal tragedy. True entrepreneurs will pick themselves up, learn all the lessons and start again, wiser and tougher.

Entrepreneurship should, I believe, be seen as a career, not the antithesis to a career. As with conventional careers, there is a lot of learning to do, and there will be bad patches when things appear to be going wrong (probably the points when you will learn the most).

I would like to conclude this section with some thoughts on how entrepreneurs actually minimise risk in practice.

First, most successful entrepreneurs follow the advice in Chapter 1; they *start small and cheap* and they *get a customer as quickly as possible*.

Many entrepreneurs I know have started businesses almost as a hobby and have grown into them. Alexi, a doctor, had a hobby of buying flats, fixing them up in his spare time and renting them out. Over a period of 10 years, he built up a portfolio of 20 properties. Then he left his job to work on his property port-folio. He says, 'I just love restoring places, sanding down staircases and returning properties to their original splendour. I had no idea it would make me so much money.'

In contrast to this approach, I can relate horror stories of people who have, on the basis of purely theoretical research or even just a 'hunch', quit their job, borrowed a load of cash, rented and kitted out premises, bought vehicles and machinery, hired staff, had expensive marketing materials created (etc. etc.), all before anything has been made or sold. In my view, that is taking a big risk. It is what, I think, the public believe entrepreneurs do. No wonder they think that ours is a risky way of living!

Second, entrepreneurs *stay nimble*. Even when the business has shape, structure and systems, they remain aware of options and allow themselves to experiment.

Third, they *plan carefully*. 'Carefully' does not mean unimaginatively or without daring, but assiduously. Entrepreneurs who are 'big picture' people, who don't like the details of planning, force themselves to plan until they can afford to hire someone and let this person do the detailed planning for them.

By 'plan', I don't just mean 'do a business plan'; you need to map out the use of all your time systematically. You should do this the moment you decide to start a business, a long time before you write a detailed formal business plan. And when you do write your formal business plan, it does not become a substitute for your regular planning.

Note that planning is not the opposite of being nimble. A careful plan can be amended more easily than a half-baked one full of assumptions. Entrepreneurs plan, but are not wedded to plans – planning is a means to an end, success, not an end in itself. I talk more about planning in the next chapter.

Finally, successful entrepreneurs *take finance very seriously* – even if, or especially if, it is a Capability Set they are initially short of. Yes, I know there are stories of entrepreneurs who are financially illiterate. These are often overstated – the successful business person who says jokily that they 'can't even read a balance sheet' is usually either exaggerating, has a business partner who is financially very sharp, is incredibly lucky, or has a natural mean streak that prevents them wasting money. They may also be better at reading cash flow forecasts than balance sheets.

Wise entrepreneurs also take their personal finances very seriously – if they're in employment, for example, they start saving, to build a 'safety net'.

Avoiding risk

- Start small and cheap.
- Get customers as quickly as possible.
- Stay nimble.
- Plan carefully.
- Take finance seriously.

A final thought about risk: we feel risk by experiencing fear. But what exactly is that fear of? As a coach, I often find myself dealing with a 'presenting problem' (like 'stress'), which then is revealed to have a deeper problem behind it ('business near financial collapse'). NLP asks 'what is the problem behind the problem?' So ask yourself what is the real fear behind your perception of risk? Is it fear of financial loss, of shame, of telling your partner you've lost money, of being laughed at in the pub? Deal with these fears – for example by talking the matter through with your partner, or going to a new pub – and the 'risk' may suddenly seem a lot less frightening.

Decisions

Another popular view of entrepreneurs is that we are decisive. The public have got this one right – but again, often in a skewed way, thinking that entrepreneurs spend their time making big, life-changing decisions.

Actually, entrepreneurial life is largely about making lots of small, quick decisions. To think like an entrepreneur, you must be able to do this. People who agonise about tiny decisions will not succeed in business; they will be dragged down by their indecisiveness; they will become exhausted by it. This is why the 'entrepreneurial chip' I talked about in the introduction is so important. It just decides – bam! – and you get on with it.

If you tend to over-agonise about decisions, consider the following:

Much indecisiveness is caused by a lurking *perfectionism*. 'OK, Option A looks fine, but is it really the best possible one. Is it the perfect one?' Perfectionism is often seen as a rather admirable thing, but it can be highly destructive. It pushes people in one of two ways. One is down into an ever-smaller 'box'. Following procedures to the letter in a large organisation may be 'perfect' behaviour, but it's not very life-enhancing.

The other way is up and up in an endless and impossible pursuit of perfection. Arguably this is a worthy aim (though the psychologist Albert Ellis built an entire, and very successful, therapy out of the perception that perfectionism is a kind of madness). It keeps people aspiring and creating. But it must be understood that the only way to this perfection, or even towards it, is *via imperfection*. As an entrepreneur, you will be starting with something very imperfect, and must accept that fact and learn to see that as a good thing. Imperfection means opportunity to learn, change, create, build, expand and adapt. As NLP co-founder Richard Bandler says, 'Anything worth doing is worth doing badly at first.'

An alternative to perfectionism is provided by the British psychologist Donald Winnicott, who studied parenting and child development. It is surely right to strive to be a 'perfect parent'? No, he found; the best parents were 'good enough', balancing their own needs with that of the child, and thus enabling the child to get a healthy dose of frustration and reality and thus grow into a reasonable adult. 'Good enough' was actually best, and I believe this to be true of entrepreneurial decision making. Good enough and quick.

I have a simple model for deciding. If faced by a choice, I ask, 'What is the worst that could go wrong?' If the answer to this is something serious, then I get advice. If there are no big consequences, I make a quick decision then get on with something else (there's never any shortage of things to do). The worst thing you can do is dither.

Having decided, I put the decision into action at once. To those readers who are 'natural' entrepreneurs, this advice is not necessary, but for others it must be stated loud and clear. An unimplemented decision is as damaging as an unmade one.

Actually, a lot of decisions turn out to be a lot less crucial than they appear. Events always move on: even the best decision can be made 'wrong' by unforeseen subsequent events (and a badly-made one may turn out to be lucky after all). As long as you keep your central goals clear, you can always correct small decisions that seem not to be working – just as a sailor on a changeable day keeps making alterations to their course to ensure they get to their destination.

If things do go badly wrong, stay positive. Don't lapse into beating yourself up. Sort out whatever problems have resulted. Make an objective study of what went wrong and why; learn the relevant lessons; move on. Be proud of your ability to do this – entrepreneurship is about perpetual learning, and if you deal with mistakes this way, you are actually doing it right.

Genuinely big decisions will need consultation. Indecisive people can hide behind the need to speak to others as an excuse for inactivity ('It's not a good time.' 'They're busy.' 'Am I sure this is exactly the right person to talk to?'). Entrepreneurs get in front of good enough advisers as quickly as possible.

As I said, much of the above advice will not be needed by many 'natural' entrepreneurs, who may suffer from the opposite, namely a desire to get to an outcome quickly at all costs – even in those decisions where time needs to be taken and experts consulted. But haste is a much less destructive failing than dithering. The clogging up of decision making, either in not making the decision or agonising about what's been done, causes much more damage. The 'hurry-up driver' of many entrepreneurs probably irritates other people, but it stands us in good stead when faced by the perpetual need for small decisions that is the reality of running our own businesses.

Luck

'Lucky' breaks are usually the result of a great deal of hard work, often invisible to the uninformed observer, who misinterprets the event as a piece of luck. Part of this 'luck' is due to simple numbers: the more doors you knock on, the more likely you are to find someone interested in what you've got to offer. And part of it is a matter of refining your skills as you do so: learning what sort of doors to knock on, and improving your pitch for when someone answers the door.

Remember that active entrepreneurs will probably encounter more bad luck than passive people, too. It's a truism (but one that is often forgotten by people who think entrepreneurs are just people who 'get lucky') that there are skills both to riding out the bad luck and to making the best of the good luck. (I cover these skills in Chapter 4.)

Nevertheless, many entrepreneurs believe themselves to be lucky people. Barry Pearson's first words (after the usual politenesses) to me were that he'd been 'born lucky'. This is a thoroughly healthy thing. The psychologist Richard Wiseman has shown that a genuine belief in one's luckiness easily becomes a self-fulfilling prophecy (as, sadly, can its opposite). In his book *The Luck Factor*, which I highly recommend, he shows that people who consider themselves to be lucky also:

■ Socialise, thus creating opportunities for contacts, new ideas etc.

■ Listen to their intuitions.

■ Expect things to turn out well.

■ Look for the 'silver lining' when things turn out wrong.

■ Believe other people to be competent, not fools.

■ Compare themselves favourably with others (not in a vain sense but in the sense of counting blessings).

■ Don't ruminate on the past but look forward.

Unlike other books on positive thinking, *The Luck Factor* is based on research rather than just anecdote. As entrepreneurs, you probably do all the above anyway, but it's nice to see these behaviours confirmed as 'luck-creating' by serious research.

So luck is something created by your hard work and by your positive mental attitude, and to turn into real success, it needs to be followed up ruthlessly. It is not something handed out totally at random: people who think that is the case are probably driven by envy.

Convention

One area where I completely agree with the public perception of entrepreneurs is that we are rebels. Not necessarily anti-establishment – that kind of 'rebel' is pretty formulaic: entrepreneurs are much more imaginative than that. I mean that we do things our way and take pride in that. We have a deep love of freedom – our own, and often that of other people as well.

When I was young, I hung out with some pretty rough characters, who spent quite a lot of their time on the wrong side of the law. What I liked about these people was their sense of buzz, of life, of authenticity. They did things their way, and revelled in the fact. Hopefully we've all moved on to be more responsible citizens – but also hopefully we have all retained that sense of life as an adventure too.

I see this buccaneering spirit in many of the entrepreneurs I meet, and love it. Even when they are being a pain – to others, to me as their coach, to themselves – there is always something exciting and life-affirming about them. Think of Steve Jobs, the entrepreneurial drive behind Apple. When the company became too corporate for him, he took off with a team of maverick techies and set themselves up in new premises, over which a Jolly Roger was hoisted. Do the same for your business!

Many social norms are outdated, and belong to an era when a ruling elite felt the need to keep the proles and the peasants in their place. Why follow them now, in the twenty-first century?

I'm not advocating a completely amoral approach to business or life in general. I am advocating that you work out *your* beliefs and *your* values and then live by them with confidence and resolution. The concept and the process that follow will help you do this.

Concept: The Logical Levels

This is a powerful and popular NLP model with many uses. It was originally created by Robert Dilts; what follows is our own interpretation of it.

One use of the Logical Levels is a simple diagnostic tool for any kind of problem involving human beings (i.e. most business problems). 'What level is the problem at?' can be a powerful way of finding a quick, effective solution.

But another, and in my view more powerful, use is as a model of human motivation. Each of the levels can be seen as a largely independent motivational system with the power to affect our emotions, thoughts, will and actions. When messages from one system contradict those coming in from another system (or systems) – which they will do, unless effort is made to align them – we experience internal conflict. The image that comes to mind is of the cartoon 'harassed executive' trying to answer six telephones at once, while down each phone an insistent voice is barking a different set of orders.

The levels are:

■ mission

■ identity

■ beliefs, values and desires

■ capabilities

■ behaviours

■ environment.

Let us look at these in greater depth.

Mission

People who are focused at this level dedicate their lives to something big, something that they feel connected to and that guides their decisions. This doesn't have to be saving the planet; an entrepreneur driven by the desire to improve the way things are done in their industry has a mission.

Some writers on business say that you must start with a mission. I'm not convinced by this. Stephen Covey, a business writer I very much admire, says that your mission is something that you detect within yourself. For a business, a mission can evolve (playwright Arthur Miller said something similar: the story grabs you immediately, but the underlying theme, what the play is really 'about', only emerges as you start writing it). A simple *aim*, to pay the bills, is enough to get a business off the ground.

In the long run, a mission becomes necessary, both for businesses and human beings. 'The good life is one inspired by love and guided by knowledge,' as the philosopher Bertrand Russell wrote.

Identity

This is 'who we really are'. It is the most enigmatic of all the Levels. It is often surrounded by, or even contaminated by, falsity – by 'beliefs about identity' which we have picked up on the journey of life. Identity is precious and often vulnerable: people will give up a lot rather than face a challenge to their identity. But at the same time it is oddly reticent, hence those teenage – and adult – years many of us spend wondering who we really are, while at the same time knowing we 'really are' something.

Identity often communicates its true nature in ways that seem unhelpful: a lot of psychological suffering is caused by people unknowingly acting contrary to their identity. It can – and is meant to – also exercise a huge power for good. 'I am an entrepreneur', said with total pride and conviction, is a wonderfully energising statement. (Go on – say it now. See what I mean?)

Identity can also be expressed as a metaphor. Aaron, a very successful salesman, sees himself as a 'steamroller'.

Another way of understanding identity is as the protagonist in a story. Who am I? The star of a movie called 'My Life'. This lies behind the TA notion of 'script', of which more later, and explains why the Hero's Journey is such a powerful process: it not only provides us with inspirational mentors, but affirms our identity as venturesome individuals.

Beliefs, values and desires

Earlier in the chapter I described a set of beliefs and values in action, and I hope that has shown you how powerful these are. Looking at the notions of beliefs, values and desires in more detail . . .

Beliefs are things that we think are factually true about ourselves or the world, but cannot easily go out and check (or, in some cases, can easily go out and check but haven't). They include hopes for the future, beliefs about what we can or can't do, and destructive things like prejudice.

NLP divides beliefs into 'helpful' and 'unhelpful' ones. If a belief is helpful, hang on to it. If it is not helpful, question it, test it – or just ditch it.

Values are statements about what is right and wrong, important or trivial. Statements containing words like 'ought' or 'should' are statements about values. There is an implication that other people should adhere to values as well.

Values can often be expressed to sound like beliefs. 'Sincerity is important,' sounds like a belief, but is more helpfully seen as a value, because it is essentially a moral statement, not a claim about how things are. Philosophers make a big thing of differentiating between statements of fact and statements of value, and we believe that they are right to do so. Hence our two separate categories for beliefs and values.

Values are often expressed as abstract nouns like 'sincerity', 'kindness', 'effectiveness'.

Desires are things that we want or need (for our purposes here, it doesn't matter which). They are not moral values – if I say 'I like French cooking', this does not imply any obligation on anyone else to like it. But they are not beliefs, either. They are facts about myself. I like French cooking: there's no debate about that; the hypothesis has been tested in many restaurants across the Channel.

I have put desires at the same level as beliefs and values because they have a similar force. Also, desires are often expressed like values – 'I value peace and quiet' sounds like a statement about values, but is not, because there is no implication in the statement that other people ought to desire peace and quiet too. All I'm saying is that it matters *to me* – so it is a desire.

Traditionally, NLP does not draw the distinction between values and desires. I find the distinction extremely useful.

Capabilities

These are our skills and 'how-to' knowledge. They can be anything from basics that we take for granted such as walking or speech, to highly technical skills such as forensic accountancy or brain surgery.

Capabilities can be highly motivational – most people who are good at something get a real buzz from exercising that skill. On a more negative side, the absence of a skill can be highly demotivating. If someone wants to do x but doesn't know how to do it, often that person will lose interest in a task (even if the task is a complex one, and the bit they can't do is only a part of it). Entrepreneurs, of course, will just go out and learn.

Behaviours

These are what we actually do, a manifestation of the skills we have chosen to develop. Learned behaviours can be powerful motivators, as expressed in the term 'force of habit'.

A lot of sports coaching is at the level of behaviours – a cricket coach teaching the 'cover drive' shot to a batsman is working at this level. You put your foot there; you keep your eyes on the ball; you move the bat through this arc ... As you practise, the action becomes 'knowledge in the muscle', natural and habitual.

Environment

This refers to our physical and sociological surroundings, the contexts 'out there' in which our behaviours take place, our capabilities are exercised, our beliefs and values put into practice, our desires are met, our identities expressed and our missions pursued. As such, it may sound less romantic than grand notions at the top of the levels – but it is of huge influence on us.

There is at least one school of psychology, 'situationism', that believes that environment is the most important determinant of human behaviour. In the 1970s, Philip Zimbardo carried out an experiment where a group of pleasant, easy-going students acted out the roles of prisoners and warders: the experiment had to be stopped after a few days because the levels of psychological and even physical abuse were getting out of hand.

Don't forget that environment should include the whole context in which that person is employed.

So what can we do with this concept? Let's look at the two interpretations of the levels I mentioned earlier, as a simple diagnostic tool and as a model of human motivation.

As a *diagnostic tool*, take the statement 'I can't start that business here'. Using the Levels, we can break this down and ask where the problem is. Is it...

- Mission? It doesn't fit in with what I'm trying to achieve with my life.
- Identity? *I* can't start it; I'm not that sort of person.
- Belief? I just don't believe I can do this.
- Value? It's not worth doing.
- Desire? I don't really want to.
- Capability? I know I don't have the skills.
- Behaviour? I could start a business, but not *that one*.
- Environment? I could start a business somewhere else, but not here.

I was once asked to coach the sales director of a growing business. The individual seemed aligned to the purpose of the business, proud to be a salesman and to believe that the company's products were good and worth selling (mission, identity, belief, value). He enjoyed selling (desire). Maybe he needed sales training (capability)? No, he had the skills. When he went selling, did he behave in strange ways that turned clients off? He didn't appear to. The problem turned out to be environment: he was demotivated by a commission structure that didn't reward him in the way he was used to.

For the second use of the Levels, as a *model of human motivation*, it is a tool for both understanding ourselves and for actively 'sorting ourselves out', reducing the interference that stands between our potential and our actual performance.

Look at the great psychological models that dominated the last century. Religions, of course, have long taught that the most important thing is *mission*, connection to what is beyond us as individuals. Among modern psychologists, this message was taken up by Jung. To Freudians, we are locked in a three-way battle between ego (*identity*), the id (*desires* – one type of desire in particular!) and the superego (*values*) (see Appendix A for more on Freud and the Levels). Cognitive therapy is based on the idea that it is our *beliefs* that control us. Other psychologists believe that having or not having life skills (*capabilities*) is the biggest determinant of our success or failure. For behaviourists like Pavlov and Skinner, our prime motive is habit – learnt patterns of *behaviour*. And I've already mentioned the situationists, for whom *environment* is the key determiner. Assume there is a measure of truth in all of these models – a sensible assumption, unless you are fanatically attached to any one of them – and you see how much interference all those conflicting motivational systems can generate.

Much of the time the Levels operate as if they were totally independent. To refine the model a little, there is *some* communication and influence between them. But only some. As a rule, where there is influence, it is 'top down', with the 'higher' levels influencing the lower ones: mission influences identity; identity influences beliefs, values and desires (and so on). 'If man has a why to live, he can cope with just about any how,' to quote the philosopher Nietzsche. But this rule is not cast-iron – Levels can influence upwards. For example, practice at a musical instrument is establishing a capability by repeated behaviours, which in turn can affect our identity and even our mission ('to make people happy with this lovely music that, through practice, I find that I can play really well').

The Logical Levels

Mission

- Sometimes called 'spirit'
- Connection with entities bigger than myself
- 'What is it all for?'

Identity

- 'Who am I?'

Beliefs, values and desires

- 'What is the world like?'
- 'What should the world be like?'
- 'What do I want?'

Capabilities

- Skills I possess

Behaviours

- Actions I do

Environment

- Where it all takes place

Change Yourself: The Seven Parallels

As a coach, I work with people to understand the contents of their Logical Levels (what the telephones are shouting), and then to align their Levels – to get the telephones shouting the same message (or at least shouting messages that are consistent). The change process that follows is about achieving this valuable end, but it does more than this. It also looks at your business in the context of the Levels, and by examining the parallels between your own Levels and those of the business, helps you understand that complex and sometimes difficult relationship between the entrepreneur and their business. It uses the Logical Levels and draws on a number of other models such as the Four Quadrant model of the American psychologist Ken Wilber – plus a healthy dose of common sense!

It is a substantial process. Take your time over it. It breaks naturally down into sections; I find one section a day quite enough. It is also what I call a cumulative process: it is to be done several – or even better, many – times, like a workout routine at the gym. I've been doing it for years, and I still find that it produces insights and frees up energy. Chris, my co-author, told me a month or so after he started the process, 'One day I suddenly realised that half the values I'd listed weren't really mine at all, just things I'd taken on board as a child. So I took them out of the list. The sense of relief was extraordinary, and I felt much more focused and at home with myself.'

It is based around the worksheet on the next page. You may wish to photocopy this one, or download our free template from www.thinklikeanentrepreneur.com. (We also have an example of a completed worksheet in Appendix C.) You will also need pen and paper or a computer to work out longer lists of goals, values, desires and identity-statements: the Worksheet is a summary of all the parts of the process in one place.

	You	Your business
Mission		
Identity	3 Top Identity Statements in order: Metaphor:	Positioning Statement: Metaphor:
Values	3 Top Values in order:	3 Top Values I want in the business:
Desires	I want:	The business needs:
Skills *Grade yourself*	Self-starting 1_____10 Practical 1_____10 Protective 1_____10 Interpersonal 1_____10	Leadership 1_____10 Operations 1_____10 Finance/Legal 1_____10 Sales/Marketing 1_____10
Goals	Goal 1: *Date* Goal 2: *Date* Goal 3: *Date*	Goal 1: *Date* Goal 2: *Date* Goal 3: *Date*
Assets *Grade yourself*	Physical 1_____10 Human 1_____10 Financial 1_____10 Intellectual 1_____10	Physical 1_____10 Human 1_____10 Financial 1_____10 Intellectual 1_____10

While the sheet reads 'down' the Levels, starting with mission at the top, when doing the process it is best to work upwards. We start with...

Parallel 1: Assets

We begin with a basic inventory of key asset types that you possess. Consider them, then rate your level of satisfaction with each type between 10 (fantastic!) and 1 (very poor).

Physical. This is about your physical health. You are the most important asset in your business. If you look after yourself physically, it gives you the strength to deliver consistently good results. You don't need to be obsessive; 3 hours of well-structured exercise a week without too much over-indulgence should suffice. It is also about your presentation: taking some time over your appearance is important, too, especially when dealing with professionals. For many entrepreneurs, one decent set of clothes and shoes is enough.

Human. It is perhaps a little strange to talk about 'human assets', especially for an individual, but just as physical health is an asset, so are good relationships with other people. Entrepreneurship can put substantial strains on personal relationships – the long hours, the focus on business. Are you getting the support you need? Are you taking that support for granted or showing your appreciation? This also covers your wider circle of friends. Dr Johnson said we have to keep our friendships 'in repair'. Are you doing this?

Intellectual. This is about your knowledge, wisdom and mental sharpness. Rate yourself not just for where you currently are, but what you are doing to keep growing these. Learning new things and perpetually challenging your intellect gives you the mental agility you will need for ongoing success in business. Are you regularly reading, researching and attending lectures, talks and courses?

Financial. Starting a business can put a severe strain on your cash. What shape are you in financially, right now? Have you enough to feed and support yourself and your dependants? Do you have any savings or access to credit?

Now do the same *for your business*: divide your assets into four categories, then rate your business between 1 and 10 for each category.

Physical. This is about your processes and physical assets, the analogy with the healthy (or unhealthy!) body. Is your business 'fit', in the sense that its processes are efficient, that the machines you have (computers, copiers, faxes, printers, machinery, phones etc.) work well, and that your premises are adequate to work in?

Human. This is about your staff (if you have any) – including you. Are they good at their jobs? Have they got potential for development, to take on bigger tasks as the business grows? Is there a good, positive atmosphere in the business? Do your people come together to solve problems or retreat into bunkers and look for someone to blame? Look outward, too. Consider the relationships that your business has with key outsiders: customers, suppliers, people on your 'route to market', advisors and any other people with significant power to affect you.

Financial. A business needs cash like a human needs air. How much money do you have available and for how long? How dependent are you on a single source of money, on a bank or an investor? Given lenders' short-term approach, do you have access to enough cash if times turn tough?

Intellectual. This is about two key things. One is what your business knows about the world out there – your market, your competitors, the economic and social contexts in which you operate. Two is your 'IP', the specialist knowledge tied up in your business.

Parallel 2: Goals

Make a list of your personal goals. Begin with major ones, like 'Start my business'. Then break these down into small 'sub-goals', tasks you need to complete in order to make the big goals a reality. This breaking down is crucially important – it's easy to have big ideas; successful entrepreneurs turn big ideas into reality, and do so a step at a time.

Having established goals and 'sub-goals', plan *when* you are going to carry out which tasks.

Finally, take your three main goals, and the dates by which you intend to meet them, and write them in on the Worksheet.

Now, do the same for your business.

■ Begin with the business's major goals.

■ Break them down into 'sub-goals'.

■ Plan which tasks are going to be carried out, when and by whom.

■ Put the three main goals and their dates in the Worksheet.

If you want inspiration for this section of the work, visit any major project. I love the new Eurostar terminal at St Pancras – OK, partly because that takes me to Paris, but also because it's a tremendous piece of planning. Every step of turning a rather dowdy minor terminus into this modern international trans-portation hub was planned and managed.

Parallel 3: Capabilities

This section uses the concept of the four Capability Sets – Leadership, Operations, Finance and Sales/marketing – introduced in the previous chapter. These can be mapped across to skills we possess as individuals:

■ general motivation and decisiveness (= 'self-starting')

■ practical 'getting-things-done' skills

■ 'protective' skills, like self-discipline and street-smartness, that enable you to keep yourself and your loved ones from physical, mental and emotional harm

■ interpersonal skills, for creating, building and maintaining relationships.

So, rate your skill levels between 1 and 10 for each of these four categories, then do the same for your business's skills-base in:

■ leadership

■ operations

■ finance

■ sales and marketing.

You can choose to practise a refinement of this section: make *two* ratings, the first the level of this skill that you and your business need, then the second the level that you are at already. Where are the big gaps? What are you going to do about the gaps?

Parallel 4: Values

For yourself, begin by making a list of your values. I find that when I work with clients, people often get stuck here. This doesn't mean that they lack values, rather that they don't really think about them – they've taken values in at certain highly formative times in their lives and then just got on with living by them. This isn't a bad way to live, but there is a danger that conflicting values can sneak into unexamined minds.

The classic list of values is that of Benjamin Franklin – I have reproduced it in Appendix B. Please note that I cite this as an example of how to do this listing, not what your list should contain. His list strikes a lot of modern readers as a bit worthy. That was how he felt; you must choose a list that is authentically you. 'To thine own self be true,' as Shakespeare said.

Next, having made out your list, write a brief 'clarifying statement' for each value, for example:

Integrity – feel right about something or say no to it.

Then rank them in order of importance. This is very important. Often people are happy to draw up lists of values but unwilling to do this ranking: 'They're all important'; 'It depends on the situation'; 'I keep changing my mind.' (Good! Keep on changing, until an order fixes itself.)

Finally, put the top three values into the Worksheet.

Now, for your business . . .

We are now entering the world of business culture. As a solo entrepreneur, the values of the business will largely be yours. You should implant them at the heart of the business – fair dealing or ruthlessness, craftsmanship or sell-'em-cheap – and they will stay there as it grows.

But do you want all your values in the business? Or ranked in the same order? It is important to go through the 'list, clarify, rank' exercise again, this time thinking of the values you would like in your business. If that sounds too abstract, think of an ideal employee and think of the values you would like this person to have.

Parallel 5: Desires

As with values, you need to list, clarify and rank things that you want and/or need for yourself. Be honest – then enter your top three on the Worksheet.

Then do the same for the business. While it is a good thing to keep a fixed set of values at the heart of a business, the *desires* of the business will change fast and – most important – away from you. As the business grows, what you want and what the business wants can become two very different things. It is essential to monitor this process.

Economic theorists say that business is there to provide what the shareholders want, so if you are the sole owner, the business is basically just a way of providing goodies for yourself. But this isn't the case – or rather, if you choose to see things this way, the business will soon begin to suffer and can end up providing nothing as it has failed. Businesses may not have desires in the way that people do, but they certainly have needs, and if those needs are not met, the business pays a higher price. For example, many owners 'milk' businesses to fund a lifestyle – and starve the business of cash in the process, so when credit suddenly gets tight or tax needs to be paid, the business hits the wall.

So what does your business need?

Parallel 6: Identity

Write a few statements about yourself. 'I am …' Such a list normally comprises nouns and adjectives. 'I am an entrepreneur.' 'I am a friend.' 'I am a tennis player.' 'I am British' (or whatever …) A few can be negative – 'I'm not a finance person' – but try to avoid too many of these. Do you really want to define yourself in terms of what you are not? Again, be honest. Your identity is about *the things you consider most significant about yourself*. Some of them may not be hugely admirable, but you have to accept that they are part of you.

As with values and desires, write a short clarifying statement for each one, then rank them in significance to you. The ranking procedure is very helpful here, as is time spent working on the list. Your identity will probably change very slowly (unless you are undergoing coaching or therapy, and even then don't expect miracles). But your perception of that identity, your self-knowledge, can change quicker – as Chris's did, via the change I described earlier. What he was ditching were *beliefs about identity* which turned out to be incorrect.

Put the top three into your worksheet. They should all be positive.

As well as your list, can you come up with a metaphor for yourself. An eagle? An oasis of calm? A glass of champagne? A raging bull elephant?

Then do the same for your business. Identity lies at the heart of all successful enterprise. What is yours? What do you do, who for, and why are you different from the competition? This is what marketers call positioning, and should naturally lead on to thoughts about your brand, which is essentially how you then communicate that identity to the world out there through the various media.

Think of a metaphor for your business's identity.

Interestingly, as human beings we are usually cautious about revealing (even to ourselves) our identity. Your business needs to be shameless about shouting its identity from the rooftops.

Parallel 7: Mission

Produce a personal mission statement.

When I am coaching people to do this, they often feel uneasy – the task seems scary and to require 'great thoughts'. I simply invite them to go back over the work they have done on the other Parallels, then suggest they relax and let a thought just come to them 'out of the blue'. When they do this, what comes up is almost always very apt (and if it isn't, then they can always do the exercise again, until a better thought appears).

When I first took myself through this process, I went away to an attractive country hotel and spent a couple of days reflecting on the other Parallels. At one point I suddenly felt inspired, and I found I could just write and write. I then worked on what I had written to craft a mission statement that served me for a long time. (Many years later, I felt the need to change it, so I did.)

I have recorded an MP3 that will coach you through the process of finding your mission – it's free, and on our website www.thinklikeanentrepreneur.com.

Note that your mission does not necessarily have to be expressed in words. It is equally valid expressed as a picture, sound or feeling. For example, one client reported a picture of a group of close friends, and now says that whenever she brings this to mind she becomes aware of the purpose of her life. From an NLP perspective, a mission is simply a 'state' (state of mind) and a mission statement is an anchor to enable you to enter that state. So any stimulus that gets you there is valid. This is what a mission statement, or *mission anchor*, needs to do:

- Be something you can replicate.

- Connect you to an aligned sense of all of your other parallels and to a general sense of your life's purpose.

When you have your mission anchor and are pleased with it, write it down (if it takes written form) or, if it is non-verbal describe it briefly, in the Worksheet.

Now do the same for your business. Most businesses nowadays have mission statements, and most of these are appallingly bland and thus worthless. Don't be like this – produce something of real value. What do you want to change? So much so, that the status quo really annoys you … Make the answer simple and meaningful. (I like the mission statement attributed to the founder of Revlon: 'We don't sell cosmetics, we sell hope'.) No business jargon, please. No 'To enhance customer experience by an ongoing platform of interrelated, market-focused initiatives …'

Unlike your business's identity, mission is for internal consumption, something private – interestingly the opposite from most people's personal life, where they often talk about mission but don't reveal identity.

You might also want to consider metaphors for your personal mission and the mission of the business.

You have now completed the Worksheet. Look through it and consider:

1 In those areas you assessed 1 to 10, where are you low?

2 Where is there misalignment within your levels?

3 Where is there misalignment within the levels of your company?

4 Is there a clash at any of the levels between yourself and the business?

A classic misalignment is a person or a company with a particular asset rated low, but no goals to do anything about improving that. Another one is a set of goals for which the person or company clearly lacks the capabilities. Noble-sounding missions or identity-statements can be unsupported by goals that are all trivial or short-term. Or a grand-sounding mission or identity can be made to look hollow by a long list of selfish desires and few values.

Entrepreneurs often map their weaknesses across to their business. I have clients who say at an identity level, that they are 'not salespeople'. Looking across at their business, the sales and marketing capability is low. Time to reinforce that capability – go on a course; get yourself sorted out . . .

This powerful exercise should help with your own personal development, cutting down the interference that lowers your performance. It can do the same for your business. Arguably most useful of all, it helps entrepreneurs understand and deal with the gap that opens up between them and their business as the business grows. We all have to learn to separate our egos from our businesses. In doing so, we create something with a life of its own, something to be proud of. At the same time, we have to be careful that our creation does not end up ruling us –

we need to cherish and protect our identity, values (and so on) too.

Aligning your mind for success

Beliefs and values

■ Risk – take calculated risks and manage them.

■ Decisions – an everyday essential. Start building the entrepreneurial chip.

■ Luck – the meeting of opportunity, preparation and ruthless following-up.

■ Convention – designed for peasants by kings. Find *your* way and follow it.

Concept: The Logical Levels

■ Motivation comes from more than one place.

■ Mission; identity; beliefs, values and desires; capabilities; behaviours; environment.

Change Yourself: The Seven Parallels

■ Examine your levels, and those of your business.

■ Look for 'gaps' and misalignments.

■ Understand where you and your business have separate needs and where these coincide.

■ A workout routine: review and amend this regularly.

04

Breaks and breakdowns

In this chapter I shall explain what you need to do to capitalise on lucky breaks. I will also talk about surviving disasters. In some ways both are similar: you need to do something radically different and to do it fast! I will explain why sometimes people actually sabotage their success, and how to break out of that trap. The change process at the end is based on my experience of time and project management – skills that come into their own when new and fast action is required.

Lucky breaks

I've already talked about the entrepreneur's beliefs about luck. We think we are lucky, but we also work hard to make luck happen. But there is also a special entrepreneur capability that neither of the above thoughts really captures, and that is how to make the most of a big, lucky break when it comes along.

First you have to *spot* it, and to know quickly that it really is a big break. This means two things: that the opportunity is substantial and that you know that it is within your grasp – you know you have 'pole position' in the race to the opportunity (or, even better, that you are the only car in the race!)

Second, you must *seize* it. Once you see the break, you must drop everything in pursuit of it.

'Once I'm given a good opportunity,' says Brian, a hi-fi entrepreneur, 'I pursue it rigorously and relentlessly. I never give up.' He tells the story of how he 'went global'. At a conference, he met a reasonably senior figure from a major manufacturer, who said they might be interested in distributing his product internationally. 'I became like a dog with a bone. I made sure that through this person I met the Managing Director of the company. I flew to America to meet the board. I kept badgering them until they agreed. Then, of course, I made sure my delivery was perfect ...'

I had my own big break after several years in the property business. One developer that I knew was taken over by another larger firm that I also knew. The taken-over company had a portfolio of properties that I knew did not fit with the business of the larger one. The moment I heard of this, I knew with that gut feel that comes with working in a sector for a while that this was a fantastic opportunity to buy: the big company would be keen to raise cash and be rid of the portfolio. So I rang up my contact at the big company and was told, yes, they were getting rid of the properties – and that the deal had already been done, at a cheap price. He went on to say that the beneficiary of this deal was an ex-employee.

This was the moment the deal became 'the big one'. I suddenly had more than one factor putting me in pole position.

1 I knew the portfolio was on the market, and none of my competitors did.

2 I knew the price.

3 If I put in a bid higher than that of the ex-employee, the company would have to accept mine, as the directors could get into serious trouble for accepting a lower offer from an 'insider'.

Time for action. First I gathered more information about the deal – all I could. I needed to know the terms, but most of all I needed to know why they had acted in this unusual way, so that when I came in with a rival offer, I could meet whatever need had compelled them. I soon found out that it was all about speed: they wanted the money by the financial half year end, which was in 10 days' time. For a moment, I hesitated – surely, it would be too late to produce a workable alternative? But just for a moment.

The first thing I did was to craft a fax to the Group Finance Director. This took hours to get right, but was time well spent.

The gist was pretty simple – I put in an alternative, better offer, and pointed out the facts of the case. The difficulty lay in getting the tone right – friendly but at the same time with the threat clear: you really have to deal with me. I sent it off with 'READ THIS' on the front, and waited for the reply, which I got the next day.

Of course, I had to come up with the goods, otherwise all my information-gathering and fax-crafting would be worthless. I got onto my bank, and persuaded them to finance the deal. I got onto my valuers and got them to do a quick valuation of the portfolio. I asked my solicitor to immediately stop what he was doing and drive up to the big company's office and effectively camp there for those 10 days to do the deal. All these marvellous people played ball, and I got the deal. It turned my company from a small player into, not a giant, but a player of much greater substance.

What is to be learnt from this story? Was it just luck? No. I had to spot the deal, and to understand quite how good an opportunity it was. I had to act fast. I had to be persistent. Most of all, none of this would have come about had I not had contacts in the two companies and a group of professionals who knew, liked and trusted me and who were prepared to put in special effort to 'make it happen' for me (not 'cornerstones' in my company, but experts out there).

I have heard many similar stories, of how entrepreneurs have slowly built their business base, their market understanding and their contacts, then suddenly have been in the right place at the right time and have leapt up and seized the opportunity with both hands.

Of course, deals like this are rare. And you only learn how to do them by doing lots of smaller deals beforehand, so the whole business of spotting, clinching and following up deals becomes automatic. The more work you can do on smaller opportunities, the readier you will be to land your big fish when it finally swims into view.

I like the story of Picasso, who was asked to draw something on a napkin by an art-lover who spotted him in a restaurant. 'It'll cost you $10,000,' he said, to which the art-lover replied, 'But it only took you two minutes.' 'No madam, it's taken me 40 years,' he countered.

Don't despise small deals. They are profitable and represent a paid apprenticeship to prepare you for bigger deals in the future. This advice is often ignored by people who become entrepreneurs after having had grand jobs in the City. They say things like 'If a deal is under £20 million, I'm not interested'. This is egotism, and they deserve to fail (which they usually do).

There are plenty of small deals out there to be done – and big ones will follow. An important belief for an entrepreneur to have is in *abundance*. Work hard and become a sector expert, and you will begin to attract those opportunities to yourself. By contrast, many people believe in scarcity – especially economists. Scarcity may make sense in theoretical economics, but it is a negative view to take in life, and is also untrue, in my experience. Our fast-changing, productive world is forever producing opportunities for bright, imaginative people who are prepared to pursue them.

Never let pure lack of finance put you off a deal that you know to be good. Early in my business career, I came across a deal but was worried about financing it. As usual, I talked to my mentor, my dad, about this. 'If it's a good deal, put in the offer, then worry about the money afterwards,' he told me. (Offers are always 'subject to contract', anyway. While you do not want to get a bad name for making offers on which you subsequently renege, if you really can't find the finance, you can always back off. But my experience is that if the deal is a good one, an entrepreneur will find the finance.)

Where a note of caution does need to be sounded is in the issue of *processing the deal*. Brian made sure his global deal was delivered on superbly. You must do the same. We've all seen pictures of pythons who swallow enormous animals like wildebeeste and slowly digest them. If other creatures try and eat things that are too big for them, they choke. Don't be one of them; be a python! One way of doing this is by taking on a larger partner.

One entrepreneur I know worked in partnership with one of Britain's largest property companies. I asked him how he 'got in' with these tycoons in the first place. He told me that he found a reasonable deal that he could have done on his own but instead offered it to them almost as a gift. They financed it; he did the deal; both parties made money. Later on, they financed bigger and bigger deals with him, because they knew, liked and trusted him. That way, he made his fortune.

Some people stumble across big deals by being employed in a sector (and thus acquiring the market expertise) and suddenly spotting a massive deal. The ex-employee in my own story no doubt falls into this category. Don't feel it is 'wrong' to cash in on this. You've earned your knowledge. But go and see a solicitor, and talk through your employment contract and what you can and can't do. For once, 'professional' caution will be of value here. But remember to go in with the right attitude. The question you are asking is not 'Is this possible?' but 'Given the law and this contract, how can I do this?'

In NLP, this is called using an *outcome frame*. I want this result; show me how I can get it. Entrepreneurs tend to use outcome frames a lot, while other people often think in terms of a 'problem frame', viewing life as a series of problems that need sorting, with no real sense that the process is going anywhere.

Another useful frame is the 'as if' one. 'OK, you say you can't do x. But supposing you could ...' It's remarkable how often such an approach yields new solutions to previously intractable problems.

Frames

- **Outcome** – 'I want this result; how do I get it?'
- **Problem** – 'What's the problem?' Sort it, and the job is done.
- **'As if'** – Let's pretend . . .

The big disaster

Arguably as important as seizing the big break is overcoming the big disaster. This happens to most businesses and is as strong a test of your entrepreneur mettle as your ability to seize and run with opportunity.

When things go wrong, don't:

- panic
- get overwhelmed
- sink into depression
- expect the bank to help
- take it out on anyone, especially your family/partner.

Instead:

- 'face the music' and work out what needs to be done
- take immediately necessary actions at once
- stay in overdrive until the mess is well and truly sorted
- find some other way of becoming cash-positive again
- explain to your family what is happening.

I have experienced (and survived) several of these. The worst was probably when the business was growing fast and I assumed this meant that everything was fine and so I 'took my eye off the ball'. Yes, we were growing fast, but I had not been growing the team, the systems or the level of management to match that growth. Morale was actually falling. Our overdraft requirement was rising. Work wasn't getting done ... As in the classic movie script pattern, it took a relatively trivial incident to create that 'awareness shift' which made me suddenly see the truth – I saw an internal email full of fury and foul language. I did a little digging, and quite quickly realised what a hole we were tumbling into.

I went into overdrive at once, with a kind of manic energy which a few people seem to have all the time, but which lurks in most of us waiting for when it's essential. It's a very basic survival energy. First, I did the actions that were immediately necessary. A few underperforming people had to go. The rest of the team needed reassurance that I was in control and would sort things out. I had a meeting and told everyone this; they knew me well enough to know this was true and they stuck with me through the crisis. I needed to sort out the cash position, so went to see the bank. They were no help at all, despite the fact that I'd been a loyal customer for 20 years. So I had a 'fire-sale' of assets to raise the money needed – then phoned the director of the bank and insisted they found me a better manager (to their credit they did, an excellent person with whom we still work).

That was essentially plugging the holes. But if a business has got into a bad state, it is because things are being done wrong. So those things needed sorting out too. All of them. I worked 18 hours a day for a couple of months, examining what everyone in the business was doing and how and why. I designed and implemented new systems for individual task management and for financial reporting. I worked out exactly what new posts were required, and set about filling those posts. Only when things were running smoothly again did I relax.

Another time was when market conditions suddenly worsened. Back in the early 1990s, there was a sudden credit crunch. I was suddenly paying interest of 18 per cent on loans and losing money. Many businesses fail at points like these, but I feel that the true entrepreneur always finds a way of scrabbling out of these kind of 'externally imposed' holes, even if they get their hands torn and/or dirty in the process.

I went into overdrive to find a way out, and managed to find a legal loophole that enabled me to take some properties back from banks that had repossessed them, and to sell them, which kept the business afloat (just).

You become a pretty crazy person at times like these, so understanding and support from your partner or family is essential. Don't forget that they can't read your mind: the best way to get understanding and support from them is to ask. And remember that you have to be understanding of them, too. At times like this, you are riding a tiger. Leave the tiger tethered outside the front gate when you get home in the evening (or at 2.30, or whenever you get back).

Concept: Sabotage

This is a strange phenomenon that can kick in when a business has a big break and suddenly starts to be really successful. The entrepreneur suddenly seems to do everything in their power to sabotage the business, to make it fail.

Nick came from an entrepreneurial family. He followed the family pattern, starting and building businesses. Then he began to put on weight and fall ill. He came to me 'to destress from all this work'. As we talked, he told me of recurring patterns in his business life (a great give-away of hidden psychological malfunctioning). He was on his fourth business. All the others had got off to great starts – at one level, his entrepreneurial chip appeared to work a treat – but had then failed, as every time he came close to success he would fall out with key people and end up walking away from the business. This one, the most successful yet, was now suddenly heading the same way. Why?

In discussions that were much more therapy than coaching, Nick revealed that beneath his family bonhomie he couldn't stand his father. The one thing he didn't want to be was 'like that old bastard'. As his dad was a successful businessman, that meant sabotaging his own businesses. But another side of Nick believed both in the social value of wealth creation and in the notion that money was the mark of a person's value – thus putting him in what Gregory Bateson called a 'double-bind', a mental no-win state where you are dammed if you do one thing, and damned if you do the opposite. In his case:

- Get rich = be like dad = yuck!
- Stay poor = fail to 'amount to anything' = useless scum, waste of potential, social parasite (etc.).

Many people find themselves hobbled by such double-binds. Some psychologists argue that they can send people mad – read the work of R.D. Laing for a brutal description of this process at work.

By contrast, very rational readers may think 'Nick was being very silly; why didn't he just sit down and get his ideas straight?' Well, that's what we did – Nick is now running a business again, confident in his own identity as himself (and never mind what dad was like: 'Dad was dad, and I'm me . . .').

However, 'getting one's ideas straight' is rarely an easy process, and certainly not when there are deep psychological issues swirling around the subconscious. The human unconscious is very good at holding mutually warring notions, and at letting them batter each other over and over again in some ghastly war of attrition, like a kind of inner Battle of the Somme. The Seven Parallels is an excellent tool for solving such problems, while other issues require an even deeper 'curse-busting' intervention – see the rescripting process at the end of Chapter 7.

Change Yourself: Entrepreneurial planning

"In preparing for battle I have always found that plans are useless, but planning is indispensable."

Dwight D. Eisenhower

"If you don't have a list, you are listless."

Robbie Steinhouse

Planning lies at the heart of entrepreneurial success. Forget images of charismatic entrepreneurs just 'making things happen' by the force of their personality. Successful entrepreneurs make things happen by planning, so that the right things happen at the right time. So this is something you should do from the moment you start your business. I have put this technique in this chapter because, though planning is always important, it becomes a life-saver when you are overwhelmed with work in pursuit of a big break or if things go really wrong. People often advise 'think big' and 'be creative' at these crucial times. This is probably necessary, but once the big creative decisions have been made, it is ruthless execution that delivers the results.

Planning does not have to be fiendishly complex. Simple lists are incredibly powerful things. I learnt this the hard (and expensive) way by going on Time Management courses. I came home from one of these and enthused to my wife about it; she told me she'd been running the house this way for ages.

Always have with you a note pad or device on which you can record tasks as they come into your mind. When you start a business – or run a home – you probably need two simple lists. One features immediate things to do; the other is a 'wish list' of projects you want to initiate.

I found that when I had mastered the process that follows, it was as if I had dumped the things in my brain into a foolproof system. This allowed my entrepreneurial chip to operate more effectively, because I had removed much of the clutter on to a 'hard drive'. It also enabled me to relax and greatly improved my health and well-being. (An example of the most useful intervention necessary being at the level of behaviour.)

Start every week with this. Don't do anything else until you have carried it out.

1 Take out your Seven Parallels Worksheet and review it. This will enable you to align your week's efforts to the bigger picture of achieving your mission.

2 Take a look at your diary for the week ahead and get a sense of how much discretionary time you actually have available.

3 Create a project list and a task list. The project list is of projects that you need to carry out, for example 'install and implement some accounting software'. But it also features each project broken down into a sub-list of the tasks you need to carry out to make that project a reality. For example . . .

Current projects

1 Install Accounting software
- Review products on internet.
- Call or email Bill, Joe and Sally and find out which one they use.
- Arrange to go around and see one in action.
- Buy software and start using it.
- Find out about training providers and costs.
- Input all data into system.

2 Attend ABC Sector Exhibition at NEC, Birmingham
- Find out cost of stand.
- Decide on stand location.
- Get banners designed and printed.
- Prepare handout packs.
- Find temporary assistant for show.

Your task list is a list of all of the general tasks you want to do: pay the gas bill, return Joe's call, buy this amazing new book on thinking like an entrepreneur (etc.).

Tasks

Call Sue to get price.

Arrange lunch with Bill.

Email printer for quote.

Finish bank statement reconciliation.

Send invoice to Megacorp.

Chase invoices over 6 weeks late.

---

4 Are there any new projects you need to add to the project list? Usually, the answer is no. If there are any, put them on the project list then break them down into sub-tasks under the project name. (The I-D-EA-S process will often help in working exactly how to break this down.)

5 Add a few of the sub-tasks from your project list on to your task list. This will turn your good intentions into actions.

6 Look at your diary: are there any 'to-dos' from last week you need to carry forward and add to the task list? Are there any appointments for this week that require pre-work? Add these too.

7 Review all the tasks on your task list and rank them all in order of urgency – decide for this week if you will:

(a) do them

(b) get someone else to do them

(c) put them off, for reconsideration next week

(d) decide they are so unimportant that you can cross them off the list for good.

8 Don't just be dominated by urgent tasks. Schedule approximately six hours in your week for important tasks that you've been putting off. (Urgent tasks must be done at once – for example 'pay angry creditor' – while important ones are more strategic – for example 'have lunch with mentor'. This distinction appears to have been originated by Eisenhower, who was clearly an expert on this subject.)

9 Lastly, decide what tasks you are going to do *today*.

I customised Microsoft Outlook to use this system and I have implemented this for a number of clients. The system above you can use with pieces of paper or a computer. If you would like to use my computerised version, visit www.thinklikeanentrepreneur.com.

Breaks and breakdowns

Big breaks
- Spot them …
- … and know that you are in pole position!
- Act fast.
- Call in favours – get the advice you need.

Big disasters
- Everybody has them.
- The biggest test of your entrepreneurial mettle.
- Go into overdrive.
- Plug the immediate holes.
- Then redesign your business so it can't happen again.

Concept: Sabotage
- People will destroy something if it does not fit with their sense of self.

Change Yourself: Entrepreneurial planning
- Execution is what business is about. Get your lists ready!

05

Building the team

In this chapter I shall discuss taking on staff, from your first employee to building an effective team. I will also explain the principles of delegation. In the Concept section I shall talk about Transactional Analysis (TA), a psychological model I have already mentioned but now wish to visit in more depth. Finally, the change process will focus on an aspect of TA: games. The amount of energy wasted by these is amazing: get them out of your workplace for good.

The principles of delegation

In Chapters 1 and 2, I presented the entrepreneur as a kind of Atlas figure, taking the entire weight of running the business on their shoulders. This is how most people start, doing every damned thing themselves. And as the business grows, that weight gets bigger and bigger. Time to get one, then several, then many people to help carry this ever-increasing weight for you. The whole process of building a business can be seen as an exercise in creating ever-increasing weight, but also in putting this weight down, gradually, always with the greatest care, task by task, function by function. Arguably this putting down – *delegating* – is the most important entrepreneurial skill of all.

Add to this the fact that you have to know how to do something before you can delegate it, and we get a kind of cycle. You are carrying the world. It grows. You can delegate some obvious tasks – but the time you save will be taken up in learning new tasks that have become necessary because the business is growing. In turn, you master these, then delegate them. The business keeps growing which makes new tasks necessary ... And so on.

The cycle is potentially endless – Sir Ken Morrison, for example, took over the family business when it was a market stall in Bradford, and grew the business to be a national supermarket chain making over £600m annual profit. This involved meeting a

The delegation cycle

series of new challenges, the last of which was managing the merging of the massive Safeway group into Morrisons, something he oversaw in his seventies. However, most entrepreneurs prefer to delegate themselves out of the story rather earlier. Their final job is to put the weight down as they sell the business and let someone else – or rather some other people – take up its weight. The entrepreneur dances away, burdenless except for a large suitcase full of money. (And, if they are a born entrepreneur, soon to pick up another weight and start all over again – but that's for later.)

Naturally, if the business does not grow, then this process may have to stop – though often a halt in growth is best changed by delegating a sales or marketing task to an outside expert.

Principle 1 of delegation is simple – always try and find someone better at the task than you are. This may not matter much at the beginning, where you are delegating simple tasks like ordering stationery. It matters hugely when you are putting in real cornerstones, experts in sales, marketing, finance and operations, on whose expertise the business will rest.

Entrepreneurs who are vain or arrogant often ignore this rule, preferring to delegate to talentless yes-men and yes-women, who feed the weak entrepreneur's continuing childhood fantasy of omnipotence but aren't much good at their jobs. Wise, adult entrepreneurs know mastery when they see it, celebrate it, and make damn sure that mastery is working for them.

The second big point about delegation is that it is a process, not a one-off activity (the cycle above must be understood in this light). Stephen Covey breaks this process down into a hierarchy of levels. These are:

■ wait till told

■ ask

■ recommend

■ do it and report immediately

■ do it and report routinely.

The levels relate to 'what happens if something new crops up'? *Wait until told* is the most basic kind of delegation, suitable for very junior people. The meaning is obvious – the new arrival shouldn't show initiative, but wait till they're told what to do. At *ask* level, rather than waiting around, they come and ask you. At *recommend* level, they approach you and suggest a course of action, which you either agree with or amend. Moving up to *do it and report immediately*, they are now empowered to take action off their own bat, but must come and tell you what they've done at once, in case they've got it wrong and something needs unscrambling. Finally, you just let people handle it, and report to you at regular intervals.

With all staff, an overriding principle of 'if you don't know what level of delegation a task is at, ask me' should be in place.

You bring in people at different levels of delegation. A work-experience kid starts on 'wait', though if they're bright can move up quickly; your new FD starts on 'do it and report at once' and soon moves to reporting routinely. Note that in both examples, you move people up the delegation ladder as far as you can and as quickly as you can. Things are made more complicated by the fact that you will be delegating different tasks to the same people at different levels – for example, an FD will prepare a draft budget at the level of *recommend*, but will be left to oversee payroll at the level of *do it and report routinely*.

'Micro-management', a curse of many small businesses, is a failure to move people up Covey's hierarchy, resulting in dissatisfied staff and an overworked owner/manager.

As well as moving staff towards a greater level of responsibility, broaden their remit from delegating specific tasks to delegating entire functions. You may begin with telling someone to order some new pens from your supplier. You want this person to be 'in charge of stationery' as soon as they can be – an entire function. (Stationery sounds piffling, but actually is a good place for a newcomer to acquire some basic management skills: they have to keep a check on a range of items, they have to deal with everyone in the business, they will have to deal with complaints and maybe even confront issues of theft.)

Be patient. When you move someone up the hierarchy or give them responsibility for a function rather than just some tasks, don't expect them to master their new brief immediately. The business world is full of people who talk about being able to 'hit the ground running', but most employees take a few tumbles. Clearly, the more senior the person taking over the function, the fewer initial slip-ups you need to accept.

Your first employee

I took on my first person after I'd been running my first business for four years entirely on my own. Faced with a mounting volume of work, I advertised for an experienced Secretary/PA to work from 9.30 to 1.30 five days a week.

Experience was important. When I found the right person, I said to her, 'I've never employed anyone before: teach me how to use a PA.' And she did. She taught me basic skills like how to dictate letters (this was 18 years ago!), but also which tasks she expected me to ask her to do, and for each task, what level of delegation she expected from me (neither of us was aware of Covey's model at the time, but she understood it intuitively). She is now one of the directors of my property business!

The best PAs know the tasks they should do and have a natural feel for the appropriate level of delegation. They are also good at reading people – especially you. They come to know from your tone of voice how important something is. They know when you are getting tired and tell you it's time for a rest (or quietly take over more responsibility until you're yourself again). They build good personal relationships with customers and other friends of the business. They are worth their weight in gold.

Being the boss: beliefs and identity

When you start employing people, issues around beliefs and even identity can kick in. Some people don't feel that it's right to employ others. They think that they are exploiting the employee's labour, that it's demeaning to work for others (and so on). These are beliefs, not facts. In reality, many people want the security and direction that a job – with the right employer – gives. As an entrepreneur, the idea of working for somebody else probably fills you with horror, but don't project these feelings onto others, or build them up into some unjustified theory about the evils of Capitalism. The power of Big Capital may or may not be a good thing, but by starting a business and offering someone a job, you are not immediately becoming a Big Capitalist.

I believe that it is good to employ people – to pay them money and to provide a good environment to work in. It is *not* good to be an unpleasant employer, to bully or short-change people. Those who feel that employing others is of itself wrong probably have a stereotype in mind of the boss-as-bully or boss-as-exploiter. When you start employing people you have the opportunity to challenge and disprove both those stereotypes.

As well as beliefs, people's identities can come under threat when you start taking on staff. Many people like to feel 'I'm one of the boys' or 'I'm one of the girls'. However, this just doesn't work if you are the boss. You can and should have a friendly and constructive relationship with your staff, but there is always a line. When it comes to a point of disagreement or contention, although it is important to listen to the employee, ultimately the decision rests with you. Entrepreneurs who are frightened of making decisions or of saying 'no' will gain the contempt of their staff and then find them more difficult to manage.

Other people have an identity as a rebel. Actually a lot of entrepreneurs have this, and this can be of huge value, allowing them to step outside corporate/institutional life and energising their pursuit of their own way of doing things. But it can cause problems if they are rebelling not against 'the system' but against any kind of structure or order. Building a business is an exercise in order, not anarchy. If you are the latter kind of rebel, an anarchist at heart, maybe it's time to ask if this is really an adult way of looking at the world – the TA material at the end of this chapter should help with that. Even the most anarchistic rebels of 1968 have now grown up – 'Danny the Red' Cohn-Bendit, for example, is now an MEP, a staunch supporter of the EU with fairly conventional views on economics.

The dangers of staying solo

If you don't employ people, the business will not grow. It won't just sit there, either: it will begin to implode under the weight of all that undone work. Some of this can be outsourced: there are businesses that will answer your phone for you. But in the end, you need other people in the business.

Helena, an entrepreneur in the personal development business always has big plans, yet somehow they never seem to materialise. One reason is that she cannot delegate. So she will go out and lunch clients, who will be impressed by her talk, but she comes back to an office awash with paper, and the projects discussed over the risotto and sorbet never materialise. She keeps going, as she has several clients who really like her and want to work with her, but seems fated to remain a 'lifestyle' business. Either she needs to accept this, and stop wasting her and others' time with big talk about future plans, or start the process of delegation.

The team grows

Don't rush into taking people on – a common entrepreneur mistake, especially with employees who are part-time or at a very low salary level. It might appear that there is little risk in taking on a misfit here: they won't cost you much. However, even a minor negative influence can cause a lot of havoc in a quiet, stealthy sort of way. Choose all your people, however humble, with care.

One area where this can be a particular problem is employing salespeople. These individuals can often be good talkers, and convince you to take them on. But remember, they will be the 'face' of your company, your ambassadors. If you get a bad feeling, don't be talked into employing them. Salespeople often sweeten their pitch by offering to work for a tiny salary plus commission. They clearly don't understand small business: such packages work well for people selling name brands like IBM, but not for start-ups.

For entrepreneurial companies, I feel there is a 'window of opportunity' for getting staff. People who are too young will often not focus on work, despite their claims that they do. Going out on Friday night and getting hammered, laid (or whatever) seems to matter more! Older people are usually too settled, expecting a more predictable life than a start-up can offer. They usually want too much money, too. An ideal age for new staff? Between 25 and 35. Before I get accused of virulent ageism, I must add that these are just general observations, and individuals will often overturn these stereotypes (for example, people in their 50s have often got over the big ego, big expectations stuff and can make brilliant team players).

No system is infallible – I always take staff on with a clear three months' probationary period, after which I can fire them if they are not as good as I had hoped, or, a much more pleasant outcome, really welcome them as part of the team.

4 Es and a C

When assessing staff, at interview or as part of their rolling assessment once they are taken on, I use a model that I have copied from Jack Welch. He describes it in his book *Jack: Straight from the Gut*. Welch, CEO of GE for many very prosperous years, had a reputation for being ruthless, but he was actually very aware of the value of people, genuinely believing the old maxim that 'people were his greatest asset'. His model is unusually simple and down-to-earth for something emanating from a big corporate: I have not found anything better. The 4 Es and the C are . . .

Energy

This is essentially about physical energy and general enthusiasm, but also about the capacity to take initiative, and about general confidence.

Energise

The person may be energetic, but do they also pass on their energy to others? Sadly, some people seem to drain energy from others, often by playing what are called in TA 'games' (see below). This person must be able to give out energy to your suppliers, customers and, most important, to their colleagues.

At senior level, energisers are the ones who create winning teams, teams with real 'synergy', where the whole is greater than the sum of the parts. The capacity to do this is very special.

Edge

This has various components for me. Partly it is about being 'emotionally intelligent'. If the person wants to get something done, do they persuade people or shout at them? Do they reflect on their actions and on the effect these actions have on others, or do they just forge ahead unaware? If they are self-critical, is it in a positive, learn-from-mistakes way, or in a negative, depressive way? Do they want to change and grow, or do they think that sort of stuff is strictly for the beard and sandals brigade?

There's also an element of street-wisdom and sharpness I look for – in a small business you need to be able to turn your hand to anything. People who won't progress beyond the 'wait' level of delegation won't be much help in such an environment.

Execute

Welch began with the first three Es only, but found this yielded a mixed crop, with too many impressive-looking candidates who didn't actually end up getting stuff done. So he added this to his list. Small businesses, especially, need 'doers'. Team guru Meredith Belbin calls them 'completer-finishers'.

Customer focus

Everyone is an ambassador for the business, whether they are in sales or the back room. Such an attitude comes naturally to some people, not others.

At interview, you can usually get a good 'feel' for how well people stack up against the 4Es and a C. *Energy*: ask if they do sports or at least take some form of exercise as part of their life. Look at them: do they appear healthy? *Energise*: you can often pick up what Sir Clive Woodward calls 'energy sappers' by the energy in the room after the person has gone. If it all felt rather hard work, it probably was, and you'd be better off without this person. *Edge* normally becomes pretty clear in an interview – the person has dressed smartly, pays attention to what you are saying and gives coherent answers. *Execute* is perhaps the hardest to spot. A ragged CV will show they are not 'doers', as may sloppy dressing and turning up late. For *customer focus*, look for good manners and paying attention to what you say.

A magic interview question is 'Where do you see yourself in five years' time?'

- 'I'll be honest, mate – not here' has a certain roguish charm, but is too clumsy.
- 'No idea' is too vague.
- 'In a senior role here' – that's the response you want to get. It must, of course, be reasonably congruent!

In Appendix D, I show a simple appraisal form I developed based on Welch's model. I ask staff to rate themselves on the various categories, then sit down and discuss this with them. 'You've given yourself a 4 for initiative – on what basis?' The outcome is usually a slight amendment of their self-marking (most of the time, people are pretty aware and accurate), plus a list of goals with deadlines and milestones, which I keep them to.

Your management style

Vast tomes have been written on this, so I won't say too much on the subject. Management is a question of balance. The 1940s movie star Errol Flynn was once talking about fencing (he was a genuine expert) and how you hold the sword. He said it was like holding a white dove: if you hold it too hard, it's dead; if you hold it too softly, it flies away. I believe this to be true of any human relationship, but it seems particularly appropriate for the one you have with your employees. If you are too aggressive they will become sullen and go into 'adapted child' behaviour (see below). If you are too soft, they will become spoilt and expect everyone else to do things for them which they should be doing themselves.

The material in the section below on TA will provide plenty of material for managers to ponder.

Pay and share options

You should always offer competitive salaries – you won't get people to work for you otherwise. I only offer a stake in the company to people at director level, who have well and truly proven their worth. And even then, the offer is to buy shares, not just to be awarded them. If they're not willing to invest their own money in the business, they have no 'skin in the game'. You need people who are ready to become real business partners.

It's great to see the change that comes over people when they are incentivised in this way: their mentality shifts from that of an excellent employee to that of an owner, and their commitment and energy-levels rise enormously. However nice this is, it is a rare event, as I do not like to lose chunks of equity in my business. As the founder and original risk-taker, I want at least 51 per cent. And as the person still in charge, I want more.

Putting in cornerstones

Cornerstones, remember, are people to whom key functions of the business have been delegated (or are in the process of being delegated):

- finance
- sales and marketing
- operations/day-to-day administration
- specialist or technical research (if relevant).

In bigger companies, these jobs are carried out by highly paid individuals. As a small, though fast-growing business, you can't afford the salaries these people want. What do you do?

Ideally, you *grow your own talent* – as the business grows and new tasks become necessary, a bright, motivated team member who is clearly learning fast will 'step up to the plate' and do them for you. The next best way is to *get someone on a temporary or part-time basis*. If they have the 'right stuff' and clearly like working with you, invite them to join full-time. In both these cases, you can raise pay gradually in step with the levels of responsibility you hand over to them, rather than having to make a sudden, vast payment to *an 'expert' coming in from outside* – which is the third option. This third option looks the safest, but in my experience is not. Outside 'experts' may turn out not to be quite as expert as they lead you to believe, and even if they are, they do not know you and your business.

I've used the two 'promote from inside' methods most of the time and they have usually been successful. Yes, sometimes a new cornerstone proves not to be up to the job. If so, you have to let the person go, then 'de-delegate' – take over for a bit while you either groom a new one or go outside to find someone to fit the role. That is another reason why you have to be competent in all the aspects of your business.

The one job I am not talking about delegating this way is that of Managing Director (or CEO, though I feel that term is a bit grand for what is still a smallish business). I shall talk about that in the next chapter.

Business partners

To conclude the 'information' part of this chapter, I should say something about business partners. All the above assumes that you are working on your own to start with. I don't have figures, but I believe this to be the case for most entrepreneurs. It was the case for me in my biggest business. Nevertheless, some businesses begin as partnerships.

I'm not a huge fan of this, but if you must go into business with a partner, make sure you have complementary skills and that it's clear which one of you is 'the boss'.

Complementary skills. I always ask people planning to partner to consider the four Capability Sets and analyse where their and their partner's strengths lie. Often the reply is that they are the same. 'That's why we want to go into business together – we both love x' (where x is usually the creation or delivery of some product or service). By contrast, really successful partnerships cover the four sets between them. Classically, a showy flamboyant entrepreneur (who is also rather good at delivery) teams up with a quiet finance person.

Being the boss. This resolves itself with the classic front person/financier pairing. The entrepreneur is the boss, but the finance wizard holds certain keys to success that the entrepreneur knows he or she can't survive without. Pairs with similar skills lack this natural antidote to 'front person arrogance' and can easily fall out.

Concept: Transactional Analysis

Transactional Analysis (TA) was developed by Eric Berne, a Freudian-trained psychiatrist. He was a brilliant observer of human interaction, with an eye for patterns of behaviour which he then turned into elegant, powerful and easy-to-use models. Anyone with the job of managing other people will benefit massively from an understanding of them. In this section, I shall look at three TA models. Due to space constraints, the look will be brief, but the aptness of the models should mean that even a cursory look will be of great use. In coaching, I often find a simple explanation of one of the three patterns below can completely change how a client looks at the way they run their business or their life.

Parent, Adult, Child (PAC)
"The child is father to the man."

William Wordsworth

From his observations, Berne concluded that people operate in three modes or 'ego-states': that of parent, adult and child.

Unlike many psychological concepts, these are refreshingly similar to what we would expect. When we are in 'parent' mode, we are re-running behaviours, beliefs, values, desires and even identities which we took on uncritically from our parents. In 'child', we revert to behaviours, beliefs, values, desires and identities that we developed or practised as children. In 'adult', we are being grown-up – rational, fair-minded, in control of ourselves, competent and generally trying to sort problems in an effective manner.

Both 'parent' and 'child' modes have a good and a bad side (or a helpful and an unhelpful side, for those squeamish about moral judgements). In our legacy from our parents is a lot of really useful stuff about looking after ourselves, being polite to others and so on – TA calls this *nurturing parent*. But there are also a lot of 'oughts' and 'shoulds' which can be oppressive if we do not examine them rationally (i.e. as adults) and either reject or accept them: TA calls these the *controlling parent*. That critical voice we hear in our mind saying we're rubbish at such-and-such an activity is controlling parent. The overweening, self-hating 'superego' of Freud's neurotic patients was essentially a controlling parent.

Our retained child similarly has helpful and unhelpful sides, reflected in our two words childish (a pain) and childlike (fresh, delightful). The childish self – overly compliant, showing off, sulky, rebellious (etc.) – is called the *adapted child*. The creative, fun, spontaneous side is called *natural child*.

When managing people, it is easy to slip into 'parent', and then to 'controlling parent', where we become bossy or superior. This can send the recipient into 'adapted child', when they will be either directly bolshy or 'passive-aggressive' (outwardly compliant but planning revenge inside). Charismatic entrepreneurs or salespeople often act from 'child': if it's natural child, that can be charming and inspirational, but it can mutate very easily into adapted child, which is a pain. Clearly, problems are best addressed and people best dealt with from the rational 'adult' position – be honest, don't score 'points', see the other person's point of view.

When I coach business owners, they often describe problems with their employees. One told me, 'This chap does the minimum; he never finishes a project and managing him is a nightmare.' When he was saying this, his brow ruffled and his voice tone became harsh and loud. He then talked about another problem employee who 'lost it' in meetings, getting angry and sometimes storming out. This time he looked like a frightened child himself, his eyes wide and his skin colour draining away. I then explained the above model: he realised that he was shifting into controlling parent with the first employee (who was behaving as a passive-aggressive adapted child); with the second employee, who was acting as a rebellious adapted child, he was responding as a frightened adapted child. Once he had this awareness and knew it would be better if he remained in adult, his management of these people became far more effective. When an employee realises 'the game is up', they usually either 'shape up' or 'ship out'.

Script

Berne believed that we spend much of our lives acting out a story about ourselves that we have 'written' at an early age, probably around age 5 or 6. It's a kind of early life-plan. This is an age at which we are trying to get a handle on both causation and identity, asking key questions like 'What actually makes things happen in the world?' and 'Who am I, and what is my role in the world?' At the same time, we are growing more separate and independent, and feel anxiety about losing love, so another question at the forefront of our minds is 'What do people have to do in this world to get love?' A story is a great way of answering these questions, especially for a child.

If we all wrote positive scripts, the world would be a much happier place. Sadly not all of us do. Some blessed individuals write 'winning' scripts, where they get love just by being themselves. But other children are sent destructive messages about what they have to do to get love, such as 'Be perfect' or 'Be daddy's broken little angel' or 'Please other people' or 'Love? Forget it – it's a tough world so be the biggest bastard in town'. (If you winced at reading one of the above, you are not alone!) On top of this destructive message-sending, children are prone to overdramatise things anyway, and also don't understand the real meaning of violence or death (watch a Tom and Jerry cartoon). So a script like 'I'll die and then my parents will love me' makes sense to a 6 year old.

So it can be tough being 6. But worse is to come (if you have a negative script) as, once written, the script disappears into the subconscious from where it continues to influence our actions, choices, feelings, self-image and behaviours long after we have moved on to more grown-up and accurate conscious answers to the questions that prompted the script in the first place. 'Script determines the identity and destiny of the individual,' Berne wrote gloomily.

Entrepreneurs are often driven by feelings of unworthiness, which in turn come from scripts that place impossible conditions on their achieving love. Often these take the form of a 'double-bind'. I have a powerful process to tackle these, which I shall present at the end of the final chapter.

Identifying such destructive scripts early on and using the process at the end of the book to remedy them can be an essential step in achieving business success. If you are living out a script that basically says you don't deserve, or are not allowed, to win, then no amount of technical skills will make you a winner.

Games and the Drama Triangle

Here are three scenes from everyday life:

1 Someone asks you for some advice. You think about their problem and give some. They shake their head and say, 'It's easy for you, but ...' Armed with new information, you go away, think some more, and come back with more advice. You get the same response. This cycle happens again. Suddenly the person says, 'You weren't much help, were you?' and goes off in a huff. You're left perplexed – what did you do?

2 You're busy doing something. It's not easy, as the task is stretching, but you're making a go of it, and learning from mistakes. Someone barges in saying 'Let me help!' They

tinker around for a bit, agree it's tough, then go away, leaving things more muddled than before.

3 You see an obvious example of bullying. You step in and tell the bully to back off. The bully starts whining about how unfair everyone is to him. Then the victim joins in, suddenly defending the bully and criticising you: you don't know what it's like to do the bully's job, you just walked in and thought you had a right to tell him off ... Again, you leave perplexed and upset.

In all three stories above, you've been roped into what TA calls a *game*. Turn on the TV when a soap is on, and you will soon see games in action. They operate via a mechanism called the Drama Triangle. People are described as being 'on the triangle' if they are acting out one of three roles: rescuer, persecutor or victim.

Note, 'rescuer' might seem to be a good thing to be, but people who 'rescue' dysfunctionally *do so without being asked*, like the meddler in the second story above.

In all three stories, someone has taken up a position on the Drama Triangle, and by doing so has invited you to take up one of the positions too. In the second story, you will probably end up feeling rather aggrieved at this bungled, uninvited 'rescue' attempt – you've been turned into a victim. If you then shout at the meddler, you become a persecutor and make them a victim – games aren't just about getting people onto the triangle, but about moving round the triangle.

And a few minutes ago you were just quietly minding your own business!

Games are linked to both script and PAC. People playing games are often in adapted child mode, and the position they end up assuming is usually the one they have in their script.

The most spottable symptoms (internally) that you have been caught up in a game are:

- You've just been in an interaction ...
- ... which results in a sudden change of mood ...
- ... plus a feeling of confusion, of 'Where did that come from?' 'I'm not normally like that ...'
- You feel you are on one of the triangle points.
- The other person is on another point.

The key in the workplace, of course, is to prevent these tiring and pointless games happening. Interaction in your team should be productive and morale-building.

If you find yourself in one of these games:

1 Clarify the situation. Many games emerge out of lack of clarity – people who start games are often very unclear about what they want, expect or need.

2 Step out of the action. Ask the question: 'What's going on here?'

3 If the other person refuses to leave their position on the triangle, walk away.

In the long term:

■ Watch out for people in the team who habitually take up rescuer, victim or persecutor roles, or who take up these roles then switch around the triangle, dragging other people with them. Explain this model to them, and get them to monitor their own behaviour.

■ Make it clear that the behaviour has to stop.

■ Insist on, and practise, maximum clarity at all times. Games thrive on vagueness.

■ At the same time, understand that everyone falls into these traps from time to time. 'Everyone' includes you. Do you rescue overmuch (failing to delegate, not allowing people to finish work before you charge in and take over)? This is the most common failing of intelligent, well-meaning leaders. Watch your own behaviour, and your feelings about that behaviour, and monitor it for forays onto the triangle.

Change Yourself: Gamespotting

Watch a TV soap, and observe:

■ where the characters are on the Drama Triangle

■ how they draw other people into games by placing these others on the Drama Triangle.

Soap characters often stay on one corner of the triangle and don't move. Others move round the triangle. Watch if the characters move or not. If they do move, how do they do that, and where do they go? (If one character moves a lot, trace their movements round the triangle for an entire episode.)

If a particular soap is full of examples, video it, and study the interactions closely. How do people set up games? Not just with words, but with actions, gestures, even expressions. And watch how other characters allow themselves to get roped in.

Once you have become skilled at this, watch people doing this stuff for real.

Watch yourself, too. Note any attempts by other people to draw you into a game by positioning you on the triangle. Do you set up games, too? Don't be hard on yourself – most of us do this. The aim is not to be perfect and never get lured into this stuff, but to do it less often and to spot when it has happened – again! And to be able to get out quickly, kindly and with everyone's self-respect intact.

Building the team

Delegation
- Choose people more skilled than you.
- An unending process.

Your first employee
- Teaches you how to be a boss.

Grow the team
- Assemble a 'motley crew'.
- The 4 Es and a C model.

Putting in cornerstones
- Experts in one key aspect of the business.
- Can any of the motley crew grow into one of these roles?

Business partners
- Choose a partner with complementary skills.
- There is still one boss.

▶

Transactional Analysis

■ Why people communicate so badly and mess each other around.

■ PAC – become aware of which state you and others are in.

■ Script – if you are running a story, make it a winning one.

■ Games – spot them early and cut the drama.

06

Entering the jetstream

This chapter deals with an area where many entrepreneurs come to grief: rapid growth. This should be a wonderful time – you've got over all the business of starting up; you're known and respected in your sector; suddenly, the business seems to have an amazing momentum, hence the metaphor. Handled right, it can be a wonderful time. But handled wrongly . . .

It is a time for big decisions. First of all, there is the decision whether you actually want to grow, usually rapidly, to the 'next level'. Many businesses choose not to hit the growth trail but instead prefer to 'plateau' out; to become a small, tightly knit, highly respected and very specialist business.

The alternative is to grow rapidly in the 'jetstream' that seems to carry such companies forward. Ironically, this is often a time to step back and concentrate on building your team so that they can deal with this new phase in the company's life. You become a CEO at this point. Then, if you choose, you can hire a CEO and effectively become an investor – time to move from being a single business owner into what is called a 'serial entrepreneur'. Or you could just go fishing!

I will end the chapter talking about the concept of systems thinking – essential at this point – and with a process to prepare you for a 'fresh start'.

Staying small

Stephen, the founder of an online retailing business, had grown his company to 20 people. He decided that was enough. 'I tried running a big business and it all went terribly wrong. This smaller business is like having my own train set. I can go into my attic every day and play with it, adjusting it and make it better and better. I just love it.'

There are many such enterprises, usually highly specialist and often with a smallish set of very satisfied customers. They are sometimes referred to as 'boutique' businesses, which doesn't mean they're based in Carnaby Street, just that they are small, expert and happy to stay that way.

Make the business nicer

Businesses that have grown to this point often show signs of wear from the journey. They may be in cramped, cheap premises with no air-conditioning, tatty carpets, using old computers. Actually this is a sign of what was up till then good practice: in the small enterprise, cash is too valuable to waste on non-essentials. But if you decide to plateau out – now is the time to make the business a nicer place to work.

This isn't just an indulgence. As a small niche business, you want to keep your best people and attract new staff of top calibre. Such people aren't going to work in grotty offices, however much you pay them. Why should they? They've worked hard to acquire their expertise; they want to exercise it in pleasant surroundings. Environment may be the lowest of the Logical Levels, but if – as is the case for many highly skilled people – their work provides satisfaction at all the other levels, then it will be a powerful motivating factor.

Clive, a successful entrepreneur in the building industry, lived in a luxurious house in one of London's most expensive areas. Every weekday, and most weekends, he drove his Ferrari to a suite of broken-down offices in a poor part of London near Holloway. These offices had no central heating and hadn't been refurbished for 20 years. Yet Clive spent 12 hours a day here – much more than he spent in his luxury home. Why? Like many entrepreneurs who have clawed their way up from a poor background, Clive believed that the business should be run economically. He was, of course, right – but now it was time to loosen the purse-strings a bit. Fortunately, he did. The Ferrari was vandalised one day, and he moved offices to a nicer part of town. His staff were delighted, and he was happier too.

This is also the time to reward people really well with good pay and 'packages'. They are forgoing the chance of promotion to stay with you, as your business is no longer going to grow.

And something for yourself ...

Many owner/managers of growing businesses live much more frugally than Clive – they have not been able to take much money out of the business, as it has always needed extra finance. If you 'plateau' the business, now is the time to start taking more out of it. In TA, a common script takes the form of 'nice things can only happen to me when I've undergone a lot of pain' (an 'until' script, to use the jargon). For example, some parents say 'it's hard work bringing up kids, but when they leave home, we'll enjoy ourselves again'. Some artists talk about 'having to pay your dues before you become successful'. And some entrepreneurs believe that they must struggle to build the business, and can only enjoy the fruits when the business is sold. There is some wisdom in these attitudes, but only some. Life isn't just a set of trials but a journey to be enjoyed. So if you haven't taken much out of the business yet, now is the time to take more. As my dad said, 'Give yourself a treat every now and again. It reminds you why you went into business in the first place.'

In strategic terms, the plateaued business is becoming a 'cash cow'. This term is taken from the Boston Consulting Group matrix, where the three other alternatives are 'star' (large business performing and growing well), 'question mark' (small business with possible potential – you've been through that phase), or 'dog' (failure – you're not that). The metaphor is clear; the business is milked for cash flow. Such businesses cannot just be left to 'run themselves', but do not consume the investment needed to sustain a fast-growing 'star' – hence the extra money available for entrepreneur, staff and premises.

A star is born

Most entrepreneurs, however, do not take the 'stay small' option. They have their eyes on the really big prize that comes with rapid growth, with potential star status. If you decide to pursue this option, there are five key questions that you must ask yourself:

1 'Why?'

2 'Do I understand the risk?' This next phase of growth is as dangerous as when you started out or when you took on your first group of employees. By going for this, you could risk the business going into insolvency.

3 Knowing this, ask, 'Am I willing to bet my business on moving up to the next level?' If not, don't do it!

4 If you are willing, the next question is 'Will there still be a role for me in this new enterprise?'

5 And finally, you must ask: 'Do my existing cornerstones have the competence to move to that higher level?'

Looking at these in greater detail . . .

1 Why?

Some people launch themselves into the jetstream of rapid growth because of vanity, or for the 'buzz', or because they have been hypnotised by dreams of having companies worth tens of millions of pounds. Unwise. The only good motives for growing are a profound and justifiable conviction that the company has what it takes to grow, and a strong enough belief that you can achieve this safely.

2 & 3 The risk

Wise entrepreneurs who make this leap understand that they are effectively betting everything they have built up so far on what is really a new venture. Why? Essentially it's about people. You need cornerstones who are expert at handling fast growth.

Soon proper HR procedures and cost controls will be needed, with all the bureaucracy they bring. And if you are not cut out to be (or don't want to be) a CEO, you will need such a person – who will want a decent salary and to install more expensive systems, smarten the place up, and generally spend money on making everything and everybody more structured and business-like. All of these cost. Can you earn the extra money to put all of these desiderata in place? Even fast growth tends to be linear, but sudden new calls on funds from expensive new people or systems come in leaps.

4 Still a role for me?

Probably not. Your old one, as head of a small team, will vanish as the place gradually fills up with people who don't know you as an individual, but who are very good at some small, specific function. Any other roles you are now playing – as leader of the finance, sales, marketing and operations functions – you are now planning to delegate. Yes, there will be a new role for you, that of a CEO, with leaders of these functions reporting to you. But most entrepreneurs are not good in this role – so you will probably need to delegate that job to someone else too, a process I describe later in this chapter. At the end of it all, you will probably end up as a kind of President figure, and maybe as an investor.

5 Upgrading your cornerstones

In order to grow your business, you will need to have an effective board of directors: a CEO, a Finance Director, a Sales and Marketing Director, a Chief Operations Officer and possibly some kind of Technical or other specialist Director, depending on your sector.

The key question is: 'Are the people currently heading up these functions in your small business capable of continuing to manage them as the business grows?' It's a tall order for them, for two reasons. One is that you intend to hand over more control to them – up till now, you have been keeping a close eye on them, with relatively few tasks at the 'do it and report routinely' level. Now you want them to take more responsibility, as you will be busier and won't have the time to manage so closely. The second reason is that the jobs themselves become harder. Getting the finances right for a fast-growing company is notoriously difficult. As is managing more and more salespeople, organising large marketing campaigns, expanding production (and so on). Someone who was great at half running, half being-watched-as-they-ran a function in your old small company might be hopeless at fully running a department in the new, fast-growing one.

And if you get it wrong ... Even if one old cornerstone fails to make the double jump up to heightened responsibility for more difficult work, this can destroy the business. Yet you know, like and trust these people. They have helped you along the journey so far ...

My experience is that most entrepreneurs know 'in their gut' if someone hasn't got what it takes to make that change. If so, that person must go. Often it's the nicest person on the team – but you cannot afford sentiment at this point. Your business is probably quite successful, so you can afford to be generous.

An alternative is to give this individual the option of working under a new, 'full-strength' cornerstone who does have the experience. In my experience this will be a fairly poisonous relationship. The truth is that businesses in the 'jetstream' grow to a point where they have outgrown particular individuals' competences, and those people often have to move on. (Remember the Peter Principle, which states that employees get promoted to their level of incompetence.)

What you do not have to do is upgrade all your cornerstones *at once*. In my view, the first one you need to focus upon is operations. This is because ops is what keeps the wheels of the business turning. If these clog up, you can forget the rest.

Next, get a real Finance Director. Hiring someone of the right calibre here will not only ensure that your own financial processes are strong enough to handle the pressures of growth, but will also reassure any investors or bankers: if things get tough, your relationship with finance providers can be 'the difference that makes the difference'.

Raj, a successful entrepreneur in engineering, had a finance cornerstone who operated reasonably efficiently when the business was at a lower level. When the decision to grow the business was taken, Raj decided to make this person Finance Director. However, the person had always had jobs such as Financial Controller or Group Chief Accountant and had never had the experience of being a full FD. He proved unable to make the move. A poor leader, he alienated subordinates. He produced simplistic cash-flow models so that the business ran out of money. A successful business with a good order book was put in jeopardy.

There are now companies who provide part-time Finance Directors, people with experience of fast-growing businesses. This makes this transformation easier – the part-timer can move to full-time as their workload expands.

Finally, there's sales and marketing. Many entrepreneurs I know refuse to hand over the sales function: they employ a sales manager, but do the 'making and keeping key contacts' work themselves. This is partly because big customers like dealing with 'the boss', and partly because entrepreneurs are unwilling to hand their contacts over to someone else, who might then disappear with them. So make sure that if you do get a sales cornerstone, this person is motivated to stay.

Enter the coach

If you haven't had business coaching yet, now is an excellent time to begin. Your cornerstones should be receiving it too.

Get a coach who has experience in coaching successful entrepreneurs. Get someone who will challenge you and is not afraid of saying something you may not want (but still need) to hear. At the same time, find a coach you like and trust and who likes and trusts you. During this transition, it is refreshing and enlightening to have someone who cares about you and who does not 'have an agenda' for you (something your staff and stakeholders will invariably have).

The rest of the team should be on a development path, too. This can partially be effected via training – for example, I sent all my team on a Time Management course, and let it be known that I would send people on courses if they asked (as long as they could justify it to me). Beyond this, I tried to create a learning culture in the company. I told everyone that if they came and asked me how to do something, I would show them – or get someone else to show them. To be ignorant *and ask* was a sign of initiative and intelligence, not stupidity. I trust that filtered down through the entire company. 'If you don't know, ask someone.'

These interventions do not have to be hugely expensive. If they ensure that rather than going out into the marketplace for new cornerstones, you can grow your old small-business cornerstones into effective growth-company ones, training and coaching will actually save you a lot of money at this crucial period. They are, of course, long-term investments, too. The long-run aim is to create a kind of 'team chip' to replace the 'entrepreneur chip': the team functions as a unit, knowing (of course) their own functions automatically, but also each other's style, strengths and weaknesses, and the constraints under which the business operates. You hear comments like: 'Jill won't accept that ...' 'Kevin will want x and y in place before we do this ...' 'Even though I'm sales manager, I know that at the moment we can only raise output by 5 per cent ...'

The cocoon phase

Usually, entrepreneurs are quite externally focused, busy 'out there' doing deals or maintaining key contacts. When these big internal changes are taking place, however, the entrepreneur needs to switch their focus to inside the company and to building really close relationships with the new or emerging top team.

Be ready for this change! You will need to take your key contacts out to lunch (or make some long, reassuring phone calls) and explain that you will be spending more time building your team and that you expect this to take about six months. Assure them that you still want their business (or whatever they bring to you) and that if they have any concerns, they must get in touch at once. You are available all the time. This may sound scary – 'Won't I lose business this way?' – but I didn't lose any business in this phase. Your key customers and stakeholders are often honoured to be taken into your confidence and will be patient if the phase does not last too long (any more than nine months, and patience will begin to wear thin).

During this period you must be very focused, clear and organised. Have a very efficient PA; keep very detailed notes on meetings; make sure that everything is followed up.

You are the CEO

You are effectively now the CEO of this large, growing, structured business. The CEO's main job is to make sure that the cornerstones do their job. If one of your cornerstones makes a mistake and you don't know about it, then you are not doing your job.

Similarly if they screw up and you start blaming them, you are not being a proper CEO. Remember President Truman's desk ...

You need to set up systems that enable you to monitor your cornerstones' performance – but to me the key to this job is coaching. You become the cornerstones' coach.

My approach during this phase was to offer quarterly reviews, and weekly meetings closely monitoring progress of the goals agreed in the reviews. Both of these were one-to-one: with four cornerstones, this seemed like a full-time job. I had a lot of coaching myself at this time, as did the rest of my team.

The quarterly reviews were the most important part. They lasted two to three hours. In them we set goals for the forthcoming three months. These goals were not only operational, but about creating new systems and procedures to replace me and to enable the cornerstone to raise their game in that area. After the meeting, the cornerstone had five days to send me a detailed list of goals we had agreed, after which we agreed a further meeting to finalise the goals. (This may seem pernickety, but it was essential that I saw evidence from them that what I thought we had agreed was what *they* also believed we had agreed.)

After a while, they started creating their own goals, and the sessions became less like management and more like true coaching sessions, where the client 'sets the agenda'. We were able to concentrate on larger, more general motivational issues – and I was soon able to stand aside and leave what was now very personal work to a professional coach who did not have any agenda for them.

Sometimes I would engineer cornerstones to work together to use their complementary strengths to improve a department. Other activities that made a real difference during the cocoon phase were monthly 'top team' meetings with the four cornerstones and spending time, also with the cornerstones, doing team goal-setting and creating mission statements off-site. A new company culture was born, and my role as leader rather than manager really came out. I found my NLP training invaluable.

Inside the cocoon, it's not only the business that is changing. You are metamorphosing from a small business owner to being the leader of a growing business. There is much reading to be done at this stage, and a philosophical shift needs to take place. Up to that point, I had been essentially a manager, making sure stuff got done. As a leader, the responsibility was wider. As Peter Drucker said: 'Management is doing things right; leadership is doing the right things.'

The book that provided most inspiration was Stephen Covey's *Seven Habits of Highly Effective People*. The idea that I would achieve more by focusing on vision and mission, by spending time reading or imagining our future, by planning team sessions and inspiring my cornerstones to move up to leadership level, by actually letting go of the day-to-day content (to quote Drucker again, 'moving from working in the business to working on the business') – all this was a wonderful liberation for me. And, more important, it helped the business enter the growth jetstream and flourish.

Hiring a CEO

Despite the above, I knew that in the end I needed to move on. It was my last full journey round the delegation cycle – master the art of being a leader, then pass that role on. Other entrepreneurs will stick with this new role and build great businesses. I felt the entrepreneur's urge to start something new – and this was not compatible with full-time business leadership. So it was time to look around for a CEO.

Unlike cornerstone-building, internal promotion is unlikely to provide such a person: you need someone who has built a business before. I was very lucky to find mine via the Society of

Turnaround Professionals. Advertise; head-hunt; get your mentor on the case – do whatever is necessary to get the right person for this most important job.

Your relationship with this person will be very close. In a way you are still managing them, but in other ways they are managing you. Ironically, my career as a hirer of people came a full circle. Just as I had asked my PA (the first person I had hired), 'How do I use you?', so I had to ask the same question of my new CEO. He told me, too.

However well you choose, there will be 'creative tension' between you. They are the expert on life in the jetstream. Your expertise remains your business: your people, your customers, your contacts, your market, your sector. Good entrepreneurs retain a kind of instinct for issues in their business, which no outsider can match. As with all such tensions, you have to be open and discuss issues in 'adult' mode. Because of this, it is essential that you share core values with your CEO. Not trivial ones like an interest in skiing, but a deep vision of what business (and life generally) is about. My CEO and I, for example, both believe strongly that 'business is about people' and have a passion for developing individuals.

You and your CEO would benefit from having independent coaches.

Leave on a high

All of the above – putting in and delegating functions to 'full' cornerstones; putting in and delegating the whole business to a CEO – is an exercise in letting go. Many entrepreneurs find this difficult. From early on, they should have separated their own ego from the business – but many do not. The ego, in its most childish form, is afraid of letting go of anything. But an egotistical entrepreneur clinging to power can destroy a business.

Most of us have some ego tied up in the business, so find handing over to a CEO a bit of a wrench. However, once I was confident in my CEO's ability and character, I felt a great weight drop from my shoulders, and became a relaxed, happier and even healthier person.

Essentially, I knew I had appointed a CEO to my business who was a better CEO than I was. I had done the same with the other functions that I had once had to do myself – even those ones where I prided myself on having particular skills, such as doing deals and designing systems. I had also created an organization that was structured in such a way as to incentivise these better people to work smart and hard and really make us grow. It was really a delight to see them at work, enthusiastic and energetic and all in the cause of my business!

What next? Some entrepreneurs sell out at this point.

Paul, an entrepreneur in high tech engineering, decided to sell his shares so that he would be able to retire and sail his yacht. He did this for two years, then came back to entrepreneurship. Ten years after this return, he now has a portfolio of about 20 small businesses, and finds this 'more exciting and dynamic' than the one business he once owned and ran.

If you do not sell, you will find that you still have residual responsibility. The buck still ultimately stops with you. This is not always a very satisfactory situation.

Whether you sell or not, you need to start looking around for future projects. For me, this was easy; my fascination with psychology and human growth led me to NLP and coaching, and to setting up NLP School Europe and The Coaching Consultancy. You should think what other roles or ventures you would really enjoy being involved in, and start making some gentle enquiries into how you could bring this about. Take some time to learn some new skillls that will come in useful in these new roles.

If you haven't got a coach, get one now, to help you let go. However you move on, it will be a difficult time psychologically. For many entrepreneurs, their identity is based around owning and running a business. If they cease doing this, and especially if they sell up and cut all ties with the company, and do not develop a new identity, they can suffer real withdrawal symptoms.

There is an exercise at the end of this chapter to help you with this, but I'd like to insert a story first – of how not to do this.

Entrepreneur X – best keep this one anonymous – had a thriving business making clothing and selling it all over Europe. He had a charismatic personality, which attracted many people to work for him. However he was not a good delegator, so they would soon leave again. Those that stayed often ended up getting fired, with X in a rage about some relatively minor slip-up. As a result, he never really enjoyed the fruits of his labour because he had to use so much of his own energy to run this fast-growing company. He became stressed and fell ill.

At this stage, his son and daughter, who both worked in the business, told him it was time for him to step aside and let them run the show. He agreed. A hotel was hired and a big party thrown, where he announced that he was stepping down. The next day he came into the office and told his son that he had changed his mind.

After that, his behaviour became more and more erratic, including being arrested for threatening an employee with physical violence. His children left and set up on their own: rather than supporting his offspring in this brave decision, he sued them. Then he had a heart attack and died: two years later, the business was bankrupt.

The jetstream can be a destructive place. But it doesn't have to be. Follow the advice in this chapter and its momentum can be used to create wealth and stability.

Concept: The entrepreneur as systems designer

As a business grows, it can be seen more and more as a system, as a set of processes meshed together to carry out all the tasks necessary to turn whatever raw materials you need (including time, talent, commitment etc.) into product and profit. So one way of looking at entrepreneurship is as a systems job: designer, overseer and, where necessary, fixer.

In a system, trouble is not always what it seems. A minor error is almost always symptomatic of something else, usually deeper. ('What's the problem behind the problem?') If a letter isn't sent out when it should be, why not? Has it 'slipped through the system' in some way? If so, the system needs improving. Maybe not a large improvement, but an improvement. If someone 'just forgot', do they need a better system for reminding themselves of the tasks they have to carry out?

Four key principles in systems thinking that are helpful to the business-builder are ecology, bottlenecks, stress points and thresholds.

Ecology

This concept is very important in NLP (which was greatly influenced by systems thinking via Gregory Bateson). One of the reasons why personal change takes time is that people are complex systems, and in any complex system if you change one aspect, the change has a knock-on effect on other aspects. Often in personal change, those other aspects can fight back and smother the new change, leaving the client back where they started. Alternatively, if the change is insisted on and cemented in place, the other aspects have to adapt, and may not be able to do so without incurring damage. To work, a change in one part of a system has to be *ecological*: it has to fit in with the rest of the system in such a way that the system adapts to it without undue damage.

Sometimes you can work out if a change is going to be damaging or not, and do something about it – make the change you want, but change B and C at the same time, because you know they will be affected. (The more practice you have at thinking systemically, the better you will become at predicting knock-on effects.) Other times, you won't know; you just have to watch the new system in action and see what happens.

A classic example of this was the impact of removing coffee machines from a business and replacing them with drinks served at people's desks. After this change, productivity dropped dramatically. What was found was that people used to have quick informal meetings around the machines and made small operational decisions which, added together, significantly helped the business. When these opportunities were removed, the business suffered. The machines were replaced and business returned to normal.

The 'jungle telegraph' within an organisation will often tell you of unexpected consequences of change.

Bottlenecks

Think of a crushed pipe in a central heating system. This pipe lets water through at a trickle; water builds up behind it; the pump overheats and breaks down. Fitting a new pump, the 'obvious' solution to the immediate problem, won't fix things at all. The new pump will just bust itself in the same way. Until this section of pipe is replaced, the entire system is useless.

A common bottleneck in small business is often the entrepreneur, especially if they have not delegated properly. The volume of work and the need for decisions build up, like the water behind that pipe. Finally the system grinds to a halt. Stressed entrepreneurs often make things worse at this point by saying, 'I'm too busy to delegate now; it takes too much time.' Helena, the entrepreneur I cited in Chapter 5, is a classic example.

I have been a bottleneck myself. At one time I would come into the office, read through a pile of letters, start dictating, get angry at all the mistakes that were happening ... A friend, Peter, commented: 'If you're going to have a tantrum over every task you do, it means you're not properly organised.' He actually booked me onto a Time Management course, after which the whole business ran much more smoothly. Bottleneck sorted!

Stress points

Bottlenecks are essentially slow, clogging blockages. Stress points are parts of the system that look to be functioning fine then suddenly snap. Entrepreneurs make great stress points. If you were ill, or even stranded somewhere on holiday due to some freak occurrence, how long could your business survive without your input? Be honest.

Thresholds

Thresholds are those moments when a bottleneck becomes so damaging that you decide that something has to change. In the story above, it was Peter's comment. Other steps can be more radical – and expensive – such as taking on a new employee. In reality, all systems have bottlenecks of different magnitudes. The issue is thresholds: when is pressure at a specific bottleneck tolerable, and when has it become seriously damaging?

Putting in systems is an art. Systems are essentially structured things, but a business is an evolving and growing entity – helpful structures can become constrictions over time. And at any time, a balance needs to be struck between control and flexibility. If you create highly complex systems to control every element of work, staff may start creating informal systems to get around them, and you end up with even less control. If your systems are too lax, there is no consistency in what is delivered and data are stored in the head of each employee. This makes everyone into a bottleneck and a stress point. Systems are there to share information to ensure that no single individual (or component) dominates the system as a whole.

Change Yourself: Planning for a fresh start

Moving on means freedom. *Freedom to* do something else is wonderful; *freedom from* your old job won't automatically leave something satisfying in its place. Golf courses and graveyards have a strangely similar look.

1 List all the benefits that you get from your current business. This could be the company of your staff and suppliers, having a sense of authority, getting respect, something to fill your time, a source of wealth (and so on). Make the list as thorough as you can.

2 Draw up a second list of all of the disadvantages of your continuing to stay in your business. These might include the risk of things going wrong with the business should something happen to your health, should you lose interest in it, should some external force damage it, should you, by trying to hold on to it, 'do an Entrepreneur X' and stifle the creativity of the excellent CEO and cornerstones you have put in place, or the many other unforeseen and unforeseeable circumstances that can lead to a business losing its value. As with your first list, make it as full as possible.

3 Now prepare a third list, of all the things you want to do and could do if you exited the business as quickly as is sensibly possible and had no more of its responsibilities. I call this a Dream list.

4 Given the unattractiveness of List Two, it seems wise to move on from the business. How can you continue to receive all the benefits in List One, while following your dreams as outlined in List Three?

Answer this question item by item (List 1 benefit by List 1 benefit). Some may be impossible: for example, if you are being paid a large salary by your business but cannot sell it, you may not be able to keep up your level of income. But at least, now, the issue is clear. You should end up with two more lists: one of benefits that you can continue to receive (and how you will continue to receive them), the other of benefits that your new 'dream' life will no longer provide, so which you will lose.

5 Now look at this last list, of benefits that you will lose. How many of these are 'deal-breakers' for you? How many can you happily adjust to? Take the deal-breakers, the things you think you can't do without, and compare it with List 2 (of negative aspects of staying in the business). If your list of deal-breakers is worse than your List 2, you have a problem. My guess is that you haven't taken on board the full extent of the Entrepreneur X effect, the potential damage that 'loose cannon' entrepreneurs can do by staying too long in growing companies. Much more likely, the few benefits that you will have to give up will seem chicken-feed compared to the hassles you are leaving behind and to the excitement of List 3, all the new projects and activities you can throw your energy into.

Entering the jetstream

Stay small ...

- Cash cow.

Or grow

- 'Why?'
- 'Do I understand the risk?'
- 'Am I willing to bet my business on moving up to the next level?'
- 'Will there still be a role for me in this new enterprise?'
- 'Do my existing cornerstones have the competence to move to that higher level?'

All the key people need to change themselves, including you. Get it right and there is a big prize; get it wrong and you may have to 'return to Square One'.

The cocoon phase

- Creating cornerstones.
- Becoming a CEO.
- Delegating the CEO role.

Leave on a high

Concept: Systems thinking

- Ecology.
- Bottlenecks and stress points.
- Thresholds.

Change Yourself: Plan for a fresh start

Have a life as well

So, there we are. The business is sold; you are sitting on the beach, having a well-earned break before coming back to get involved in a small engineering business, a charity you feel particularly strongly about, to master tai-chi and to read the complete works of Dickens (or whatever your dreams were). Well done!

However, it's worth considering how many nice things you can have for yourself while you are still making the journey of entrepreneurship. The 'work like a slave for x years, then you can finally have some goodies' storyline is not a God-given truth about life but a TA script – an artificial storyline imposed on us by our younger selves, who in turn had it imposed on them by an adult suffering the same delusion. As Eric Berne said, 'some people spend all their lives waiting for Santa'.

I'm not saying 'don't work hard'. You must work hard to build a successful business. But you can also stop occasionally to smell the flowers (and, more generally, enjoy the journey). A compulsive desire to 'work hard' can be useful to pull ourselves out of poverty or mediocrity, but once we have done that, it can turn on us and destroy us – our health, our family life and even the businesses we created to get us there in the first place. Don't let it.

As a coach I have worked with many entrepreneurs who worked too hard and became workaholics. Ling, a successful entrepreneur once told me proudly, 'I never get to the office before 5.30 a.m.!' Such people are almost always driven by the wrong motive.

We should work hard because it is an expression of our creativity, our uniqueness, our energy, our soul. 'Man is a heroic being,' said Ayn Rand, 'with productive achievement as his noblest activity.' OK, and to make decent money, too. We should not work hard from some hidden psychological compulsion.

Healing the adapted child

Remember the material on Transactional Analysis, especially that subsection of ourselves called the adapted child. This is a left-over from times when, as children, we were basically cowed into behaving in ways that weren't authentic or, in the long run, helpful. The weapon used to cow us was probably not the threat of violence, but the psychological weapon of withdrawing love – or, more subtly, of giving love conditionally.

So many of my coaching clients come across a message hidden deep in their psyche: 'You are only lovable if . . .' And a lot of the time, the 'if' condition is that they work hard. As we grow up, this can remain a belief ('I'm only lovable if I work hard') or, worse, part of our identity ('deep inside, I am unlovable') supported by a belief ('but if I work hard I can keep this hidden').

This turns into a toxic, negative double-bind. I've already mentioned this phenomenon, but to remind you, it is a 'damned if you do and damned if you don't' mindset. One 'arm' of the double-bind says 'If I don't work hard, I'll be unlovable', while the other says 'You have to work hard, even if it leaves you no time for loving relationships'.

Gemma was a very successful owner of a publishing business, having worked her way up through one of the world's largest publishing organisations before starting her own company. However, she was involved in what appeared to be a very abusive relationship, tolerating appalling behaviour from her boyfriend. At the end of a long coaching session, Gemma told me that her father was very cold to her and was very determined for her to succeed. She therefore had created for herself the following negative double-bind: 'If you work so hard all day long that you have no time for anything else, then you will be worthy. If you don't work hard you are unlovable.' This creates a great deal of personal unhappiness, but is also bad for business.

The workaholic's approach is not motivated by what needs to be done for the business. It is motivated by a need to feel valuable. From a leadership perspective, this can be very negative. You won't delegate. You will make strategic errors, as your work, work, work focus keeps you chained to the coal-face and does not enable you to take a step back and see things in context. You will become a stress point – then get ill. With nobody else allowed to know how the business really functions, the team will do their impression of headless chickens.

What is the solution to this? Several things. One is to set yourself clear personal wealth goals. These will essentially force you to stop working, working, working when you have reached them. Second solution is to get a coach. Third, I have a curse-busting change process which I do with my clients, and which can be extremely powerful. So powerful, in fact, that it is the note on which I shall end the book.

Know when you've won

'I won't be happy till I'm rich.'

I've heard that from several clients. Some of these are already rich. So I ask them what they mean by rich, and they answer that they don't know exactly, but they'll know when they get there. This sounds reasonable, but it is not, because usually people who say this never do know, until the heart attack comes along and tells them that the game is over.

One aspect of coaching is to get people to commit themselves to clear, measurable goals. You can't force these onto people: they have to decide themselves. But then the coach has to hold the person to their commitment. You can do this to yourself.

Having agreed these goals with yourself, don't sabotage them by changing them radically. I know of one hugely successful multimillionaire who sold his business for around £100,000,000 – and is now very upset by the fact that he has fallen in with some billionaires and feels very inferior. His yacht is half the size of theirs; he only has a flat in Monaco not a house ... Such nonsense is, of course, psychological: this person still has a compulsion to compare himself unfavourably with others. A therapist would help him a lot more than the £900,000,000 or so needed to get him into the billionaire bracket.

Business success is a strange phenomenon; it is something that happens to very different sorts of person. Some entrepreneurs believe 'life is tough and you gotta fight to get your piece of the pie'. Others believe that life is abundant and that generosity and a pursuit of excellence will deliver success. As a coach I have heard both views. It does not seem to make that much difference to how much money you accumulate. I know which one I prefer to live by – though if you take the 'nice guy' route, make sure your protective capabilities are strong.

Change Yourself: The rescripting process

"Close the show and put a whole new show on the road."

Eric Berne

This process does not need to be done in one sitting. Sometimes it is good to have a break at step 4 and start the process again the following day.

This is best done on your own or with a qualified coach.

1 You are going to tell a story. An old story. This story is best told in the 3rd person (in other words, as 'he did x', 'she did y') – even though it is essentially about yourself and your family. (The point of using the 3rd person is to get more

perspective: this way, you see yourself as just one of the players in a bigger family drama.) Choose a *name* for your 'protagonist', the central person in the story. Some people just choose a name they like. Others select a more obvious hero figure. I've had several James Bonds, plenty of Winston Churchills and, oddly enough, lots of Dorothys (Wizard of Oz), the latter often from tough-looking, high-flying male executives, for whom the name seems to give them permission to go back to a skill they left behind in childhood, that of entering into a story. That's the point of the name you choose; it must be one that enables you to tell a story about that person (which is really about *you*: if you choose Madonna as a name, you don't want to begin with 'Her first hit was in April 1982 . . .' It's about you.)

2 Now *tell the story*. If you're doing this on your own, get a piece of paper and start writing. Don't plan or ponder, just get on and do it (you are allowed to go back and change it while you are telling it – 'No, actually, Juliet's mum didn't do that, she did this...'). Don't feel the need to entertain. Just let it flow. Start with your grandparents (maternal or paternal), then your parents, then you, right up to the present day.

When telling each character's story, try and 'get inside their skin'; see it from their point of view – how they felt not just what they did. You probably don't know how your parents or grandparents felt at the important moments in their lives; telling this story gives you permission to imagine that you do – it's the NLP 'as if' frame at work.

The style of the story is up to you. Most people try and keep it quite simple and biographical. Others go overboard and use magic or metaphor. 'Dorothy's grandparents were born in a wood and lived contentedly until Dorothy's grandfather went to the war and never came back . . .' is fine, even if they actually lived in Luton. There will be a message behind the 'wood' metaphor: ask yourself what message.

3 When the story is finished – at the present day – and you are satisfied with it, *give it a title*. This title is usually verbal, but doesn't have to be. It can be a recalled sound or a smell or anything, as long as that recall is firmly associated in your mind with the story (in other, NLP words, as long as it's an anchor for the story).

4 Answer this question: 'Every family has a *curse*; what is yours?' It'll be there, in the story. This curse is best kept simple, and ideally phrased as a double-bind (damned if you do, and damned if you don't: 'If you work hard, you have no time for love; if you don't work hard you are unlovable'). It may be that one 'arm' of the double-bind comes from one parent, and the other from the other parent – but this is not always the case.

5 Spend some time *refining this curse*. Brainstorm it a little. Don't be afraid to make it as nasty as possible – remember the point of this process is to free yourself from its power, and to do this you need to confront it at its worst, most powerful, most threatening and most disabling.

6 Identify the *positive intention of your curse*. This is a crucial part of the process. In NLP, we regard the unconscious as essentially helpful but not very good at updating itself or at communicating. Even the most apparently dysfunctional behaviours, beliefs or values have some kind of twisted helpfulness about them. What about this curse, if looked at obliquely, is helpful to you now? Or, if the answer to that is 'nothing', what was once helpful in the past? Normally, in at least one of the 'arms' of the curse, there is something. In the example above, 'If I don't work hard I am unlovable' is a powerful motivator to work hard, which produces material success.

7 Put whatever good there is from the curse (however much this good is outweighed by the negative stuff) into a *metaphor*. Be as fanciful as you like: a key, a magic pen, a picture of an eagle, the sound of the sea, even a feeling somewhere inside you. You will use this to take the positive qualities that you have got out of your curse and carry them forward into the future, leaving behind the destructive, dysfunctional, outdated bits of it.

8 Now start a *new story* for your character, starting with the present, working forward to a point where the curse is transformed. The metaphor of the positive qualities that you want to bring forward can be part of this transformation (but doesn't have to be). As with the old story in section 2, you can be literal or metaphorical – I find people tend more to metaphor in this, new story, but you don't have to suddenly turn from a biographer into a mythologist. 'And then Galahad entered into the cave and pulled the sword from the glassy pond and suddenly everything changed; there was a clearing, the cave disappeared and he was in a beautiful, sun-drenched field where a beautiful maiden took him by the hand and led him to a place of comfort and tranquillity.' Great! 'Joanna said to her mother, "I'm not going to live the way you wanted me to; it's not who I am. I'm sorry." And her mother just smiled and said "that's fine; I understand".' That's great, too. Whatever works for you.

9 Summarise this feeling of your new, happy ending into a simple statement. A *motto* of some kind often works (it may be one you subsequently find to be right at the top of your list of beliefs, or your identity or even your mission). 'To love and be loved is to be truly free.' 'Do unto others as you would have done unto you.' If you can, make this motto a rephrased version of one arm of the curse. One colleague I worked with from a military background found his curse included the belief 'real men kill people'. Changing that to 'real men lead real lives' made a substantial change to his life.

10 *Get rid of the old curse.* Imagine it as an object – metaphors like 'dry old stick', 'sloughed-off snakeskin' are common. Then

imagine yourself picking it up and throwing it into the past. As with the Hero's Journey, imagine a 'timeline' with past, present and future mapped onto the physical space around you, and throw the curse there. Make throwing a powerful, memorable gesture. Note your reactions to this: is there something stopping you doing it? Consider what, exactly. Work on this.

11 *Recall your new motto.* Imagine it as an object (a sign with the words on will do; something more metaphorical if you wish). Imagine that you are holding it firmly and confidently, right here, right now. Then propel it out into your future as well, so that you can live it now and onwards for the rest of your life. Again, throw it into a real physical space on your timeline using a powerful, memorable gesture.

12 Lastly, *put the new motto into your present.* Often people are happy to accept their new story in the future, but reluctant to grab hold of it right now. But the future hasn't happened yet and may never happen. Putting the motto into the present means you have to live it now. You know how to do this, just do it! If this throws up a few more issues, then maybe the curse still has some value to you or you need to add more ingredients into your step 7 metaphor. Go back to step 6 and proceed again from there.

Many of my clients feel a huge release if they work through the above process with intensity and commitment. I believe very strongly that maturity is about 'having one's cake and eating it too' – we can and should be able to use, and enjoy using, the positive qualities of ambition or drive without the need for compulsive, irrational behaviours. Speaking personally, the ability to wake up in the morning and to be happy and content as well as being highly effective and successful is my greatest achievement, far more than the material achievements that I made during the development of my business.

Have a life as well

- Enjoy the journey.
- Hard work for the wrong motive can harm the business as well as you.
- The curse of the double-bind.
- Know when you've won.

Rescripting

- Put a whole new show on the road.

Conclusion

I wish you success, both on your journey of personal development and your journey of entrepreneurship. I hope that I have shown in this book that the two are closely linked, and that you will find the change processes I have introduced of use on both journeys. Business success is not incompatible with a happy positive life, whatever ancient double-binds may tell us. In fact, the opposite is often true: progress on one of these journeys often leads to progress in the other. The skills we acquire, to think like an entrepreneur, enable us to take control of our lives as well as our careers, and 'build the good life'.

This good life is not just for ourselves. Our personal journey enables us to create a pleasant environment for our family and friends, and to contribute to our communities and society in general. Our entrepreneurial journey creates wealth for our business's owners and value for our customers. It provides work for our employees, and more, a chance for them to grow and develop (a chance they are much less likely to encounter battling up the corporate ladder). A fast-growing entrepreneurial business creates a stream of opportunities for bright people who are eager to learn and to embrace new responsibilities.

As you make your entrepreneurial journey, remember to value all the things you are doing, both for yourself and for others. Whatever you achieve, it is something to be proud of. In an increasingly impersonal world, you have stepped out of the rut and stood up for something special and individual. By doing so, you have made the world a bigger, brighter and nicer place. May your efforts bring you the success you deserve.

Appendix A

The Logical Levels, Maslow and Freud

It is interesting to compare Robert Dilts' Logical Levels with the work of two great psychologists of the last century, Abraham Maslow and Sigmund Freud.

Maslow is best known for his Hierarchy of Needs. This consists of the following:

Self-actualisation – realising potential, self-fulfilment, personal growth, 'peak experiences'.

Esteem – self-esteem, status, achievement, mastery, independence, responsibility.

Belongingness and Love – relationships, family, work colleagues, friends.

Safety – protection from danger, elements etc., 'law and order', boundaries.

Biological and Physiological – air, food, drink, warmth, sex, sleep, etc.

People often comment on the similarity between this hierarchy and the Logical Levels. However, there is one crucial difference between the two. Maslow believed we spent most of our time filling the 'lower' aspects of the hierarchy (food, security, sex etc.) and *only when these were satisfied* did we move on to 'higher' things. He believed that few people actually got to 'self-actualisation'. In the Logical Levels model, we are driven by all the levels all the time. *In extremis* Maslow may be right – faced with a choice between food and self-actualisation, the starving person will most likely go for the food – but I do not believe this to be the case in everyday life. Hence the importance of aligning the contents of each of our levels to get rid of inner conflict.

Freud believed that the unconscious mind was the driving force behind human behaviour. NLP prefers to talk of the subconscious mind, but the difference is somewhat academic. Both operate 'out of awareness' and affect what we think, do, say, feel (and so on).

It is obvious – to anyone, not just Freudians or NLP devotees – that most of what goes on in our mind is sub- (or un-)conscious: basic body functions like breathing, as well as all those skills like walking, holding a spoon (etc.) which we 'do without thinking' (i.e. do without *consciously* thinking). Our creativity comes from down there – in art, but also in everyday life, each time we have to make choices of words or actions (i.e. the whole time). 'The words just popped into my head ...'

The conscious mind, though a wonderful thing that gives us choice and power over our actions, is a much smaller entity than the unconscious. For example, George A. Miller, a professor at Princeton, has shown that conscious memory can only handle about seven bits of information at a time. I like to think of the conscious mind as being like the thin crust of rock that covers the huge, fiery mantle and core of the earth.

The difference between the NLP view and that of Freud is that he saw the subconscious as a dangerous, wilful demon plotting against our good intentions, while in NLP we look on it much more favourably. It is, we believe, always trying to help us, even when it appears to act in bizarre ways. (See section 6 of the rescripting process exercise on p. 157.) The bizarreness of the unconscious mind's response comes from its three big weaknesses:

1 It stores things from the past with remarkable fidelity. It won't change these unless it is in some way asked to. So

decisions we made about ourselves or the world at age 5 will just sit there until we find a way of challenging them.

2 It doesn't communicate directly with our conscious mind. It doesn't know how to. A lot of NLP is about giving the unconscious mind tools to make itself a bit clearer to the conscious mind, and about using the conscious mind to 'reprogramme' the unconscious.

3 It seems to store information in 'silos' that don't communicate with each other all that well – hence the conflict between the Logical Levels.

Where NLP – and I – agree with Freud is that the sub/unconscious mind is dynamic, active and powerful. It is the most potentially effective ally our conscious selves could wish for – if we help it to be, which is what much of NLP and many of the change processes in this book are about.

Appendix B

Benjamin Franklin's 13 Values

Franklin was a remarkable individual. He was an author, revolutionary, scientist, public servant and diplomat. He was a prolific inventor, coming up with the lightning rod, a musical instrument that played tunes by rubbing glasses filled with different amounts of water, bifocal glasses, a particularly efficient type of stove, and a flexible urinary catheter. He was also, of course, one of the Founding Fathers of the USA (one of history's more successful start-ups!)

He apparently created his value list at the age of 20, and claimed to have lived by it for the rest of his life (though he did father an illegitimate child, which perhaps doesn't square too well with Value 12!) The list may strike twenty-first century readers as a little worthy, but it is the work of a principled and highly effective man – and a great example of how to do the Values exercise in the Seven Parallels process.

1 Temperance
   Eat not to Dullness. Drink not to Elevation.

2 Silence
   Speak not but what may benefit others or yourself. Avoid trifling Conversation.

3 Order
   Let all your Things have their Places. Let each Part of your Business have its Time.

4 Resolution
   Resolve to perform what you ought. Perform without fail what you resolve.

5 Frugality

Make no Expence but to do good to others or yourself [i.e. Waste nothing].

6 Industry

Lose no Time. Be always employed in something useful. Cut off all unnecessary Actions.

7 Sincerity

Use no hurtful Deceit.

Think innocently and justly; and, if, you speak, speak accordingly.

8 Justice

Wrong done, by doing Injuries or omitting the Benefits that are your Duty.

9 Moderation

Avoid Extremes. Forbear resenting Injuries so much as you think they deserve.

10 Cleanliness

Tolerate no Uncleanness in Body, Clothes or Habitation.

11 Tranquillity

Be not disturbed at Trifles, or at Accidents common or unavoidable.

12 Chastity

Rarely use Venery but for Health or Offspring; Never to Dullness, Weakness, or the Injury of your own or another's Peace or reputation.

13 Humility

Imitate Jesus and Socrates.

Appendix C

The Seven Parallels in action

The most common use of the Parallels is by an entrepreneur working on their own. But the Parallels can also be usefully used in larger organisations – such as a growing 'jetstream' business – for a range of benefits:

■ To help team members spot their own internal 'gaps' and misalignments.

■ To help team members understand where they fit well into the organisation and where they don't.

■ To get across an organisational mission or identity in a way that actually means something to individuals.

■ To get feedback from team members about how they see the business.

Working on your own at the Parallels is best done as a slow, private, reflective exercise. In this example, it is done quickly and publicly within an organisation to produce the above.

First, I ask each member of the team to fill in the Worksheet. It is clearly understood that the left-hand side will be confidential (if people want, they can fold the sheet down the middle and only reveal the 'public' half). Then we work our way up the right-hand side, finding out what everyone has put and coming to a 'group' decision of where the business actually is on the various criteria.

When discussing Goals, I list all goals. These can then be prioritised, and all the goals agreed in the session are put into the box. The process of summarising goals in writing and putting dates is simple, powerful but often neglected. When working with an organisation, I add to 'Goal' and 'Date' a line stating which individual is responsible for that goal – not an issue for the solo entrepreneur or the very small entrepreneurial organis-ation, where the answer will always be 'me, the entrepreneur'!

On the Capabilities parallel, people in charge of a function usually grade the business higher on that function than everyone else. This provides a forum for people to challenge 'gaps' in a specific capability of the business, without attacking the identity of the individual who heads up that section. However, the session should be facilitated by someone experienced at keeping things this way, ensuring that discussions remain objective.

On Values another list will emerge. This should feature a top value for each individual attending the meeting, and will create for that individual a real sense of being understood and acknowledged. Allow each person the time they need to explain their top value. Once this list is complete, it is a good idea to select three agreed core values from it. There are usually obvious contenders. One of these is 'making money', and people should not be ashamed of this!

Identity often generates the most interesting discussion. If necessary, give people time to break out into sub-groups. If ideas are thin on the ground, try the old 'If our business were an x (fruit, car, flower etc.), what would it be?' question. This is important work: you are trying to create a positioning statement for the business, which should be simple and brief, and should explain what you do and why you are different.

Finally come up with a Mission. This should flow naturally from the agreed values and the positioning statement.

This use can be extended to anyone wanting to consider their role in some larger unit than themselves, such as a family.

On the next page, I show a model Worksheet filled in by an imaginary entrepreneur with an imaginary small business.

	You	Your business
Mission	'Be the change you wish to see in the world' (Mahatma Gandhi)	Build wealth, share wealth
Identity	3 Top Identity Statements in order: Work, Friend & Family Metaphor: a Runner	Positioning Statement: The fastest and friendliest x company Metaphor: Mercury, the 'winged messenger'
Values	3 Top Values in order: Freedom Integrity Compassion	3 Top Values I want in the business: Honesty Professionalism Meritocracy
Desires	I want: Freedom and Love	The business needs: Six months of cash reserves
Skills Grade yourself	Self-starting 1_____x____10 Practical 1_____x____10 Protective 1____x_____10 Interpersonal 1_____x_10	Leadership 1_____x__10 Operations 1_____x_10 Finance/Legal 1_____x___10 Sales/Marketing 1____x_____10
Goals	Goal 1: Save £20k Date: 1 August Goal 2: Get married Date: 12 October Goal 3: 3 hours exercise a week Date: 1 May next year	Goal 1: Launch new product in Spain Date: 15 May Goal 2: Secure long-term financing Date: 12 June Goal 3: Finish budget Date: 1 November
Assets Grade yourself	Physical 1_____x____10 Human 1_____x____10 Financial 1___x_____10 Intellectual 1_____x_10	Physical 1____x_____10 Human 1__x_____10 Financial 1_____x___10 Intellectual 1_____x___10

Appendix D

A Model Staff Assessment Form

	How is behaviour demonstrated? Give specific examples.
Replace Me ☐ ☐ ☐ ☐ 1 2 3 4	
Customer Focus ☐ ☐ ☐ ☐ 1 2 3 4	
Energy	How is behaviour demonstrated? Give specific examples.
Vigour/Enthusiasm ☐ ☐ ☐ ☐ 1 2 3 4	
Initiative ☐ ☐ ☐ ☐ 1 2 3 4	
Confidence ☐ ☐ ☐ ☐ 1 2 3 4	
Energise	How is behaviour demonstrated? Give specific examples.
Mentoring others ☐ ☐ ☐ ☐ 1 2 3 4	
Leadership ☐ ☐ ☐ ☐ 1 2 3 4	

Creating synergy ❏ ❏ ❏ ❏ 1 2 3 4	
Edge	How is behaviour demonstrated? Give specific examples.
Political Acumen ❏ ❏ ❏ ❏ 1 2 3 4	
Strength/softness ❏ ❏ ❏ ❏ 1 2 3 4	
Eagerness to learn ❏ ❏ ❏ ❏ 1 2 3 4	
Execution	How is behaviour demonstrated? Give specific examples.
Identify & **Clarify Issues** ❏ ❏ ❏ ❏ 1 2 3 4	
Prioritisation & **Planning** ❏ ❏ ❏ ❏ 1 2 3 4	
Delivery ❏ ❏ ❏ ❏ 1 2 3 4	

The 'Replace Me' box at the top is about the amount of work this person has taken off my (the entrepreneur's) shoulders.

The Strength/softness box is about the balance the person has between these two qualities, both of which are important in the workplace.

Recommended reading

NLP

The Way of NLP (2001) – Ian McDermott and Joseph O'Connor (Thorsons)
A clear overview of NLP presuppositions, principles and techniques. They've written a few other books together which have a pretty similar structure.

NLP Workbook (2001) – Joseph O'Connor (Thorsons)
A useful add-on to the above, containing activities to 'embed' the learning of NLP (and to show how much fun it can be and what huge benefits are possible for those who actually get up and do this stuff).

Teach Yourself NLP (2004) – Amanda Vickers and Steve Bavister (Teach Yourself Books)
Another good introductory text.

Sleight of Mouth (1991) – Robert Dilts (Meta Publications)
A classic. The content is incredibly powerful, and will help beginners understand why NLP is not just a passing fad, but continues to be of such great service in freeing and enriching people.

The Structure of Magic I (1975) and II (1989) – Richard Bandler and John Grinder (Science Behaviour Books)
This is hard to read, but is the original work that started off NLP. It goes into great detail on the use of language, how language reflects internal reality, and patterns that can be applied for change.

Transactional Analysis

Born to Win: 25th Anniversary Edition (1996) – Muriel James and Dorothy Jongeward (De Capo Press)
An excellent introduction to TA, with a dose of Fritz Perls (one of the original models for NLP) thrown in. This book has particularly useful exercises at the end of each chapter.

What Do You Say After You Say Hello? (1975) – Eric Berne (Corgi Books)
Demonstrates how our 'life script' gets written, how it works and, more important, how anyone can improvise or change their script to make a happy ending.

Games People Play: The Psychology of Human Relationships (2004) – Eric Berne (Ballantine Books). 1st edn (Deutsch), 1964.
The classic work on TA 'games', written in Berne's sharp, lucid style.

Scripts People Live: Transactional Analysis of Life Scripts (1994) – Claude Steiner (Grove Press)
Another classic work on life scripts by a clinical psychologist (the style is very seventies, man, which can be off-putting, but the material remains excellent).

Business/Other

The Art of the Start (2004) – Guy Kawasaki (Portfolio Hardcover)
Aimed at high-tech entrepreneurs, but has excellent material for anyone setting out on the entrepreneurship journey.

The Beermat Entrepreneur (2002) – Mike Southon and Chris West (Prentice Hall)
A clear, step-by-step introduction to entrepreneurship – and it also has a sense of humour. The model of the entrepreneur and four cornerstones has influenced the I-D-EA-S process – but as competencies, not individuals.

Sales on a Beermat (2005) – Mike Southon and Chris West (Random House Business Books)

Finance on a Beermat (2006) – Mike Southon and Chris West (Random House Business Books)

Marketing on a Beermat (2008) – Chris West (Random House Business Books)
Three simple guides to basic capability sets, in clear English and aimed squarely at new and small businesses. It is particularly important to read the finance book, unless you come from a finance background.

Seven Habits of Highly Effective People (1989) – Stephen Covey (Free Press)
An excellent framework for the change from a managerial or deal-making mentality to thinking like a true leader. Also available – and highly recommended – on audio.

How To Get Rich (2006) – Felix Dennis (Ebury Press)
This book has done for business literature what Alan Clarke's Diaries did for politics. A no-punches pulled look at entrepreneurship, from someone who has been there, done that and got a rather stained T-Shirt. The honesty of this book provides some 'home truths' that are essential.

The Fifth Discipline (2006) – Peter Senge (Doubleday Business)
Though this is essentially aimed at people in corporates, this book is full of good material for businesses of all sizes. Written by an MIT professor with a new-age outlook, it is particularly strong on systems thinking.

A Brief History of Everything (1996) – Ken Wilber (Shambhala)
A series of original views on many controversial topics, including the gender divide, multiculturalism, liberation movements and the conflict between various approaches to

spirituality. Its question-and-answer format makes it both readable and accessible, despite the intensity of the material.

Online

Please visit our site, www.thinklikeanentrepreneur.com. This has free downloads associated with this book, as well as new material and information about new products, courses, talks and ideas.

To contact Chris, email him at chris@chriswest.info or visit his site www.chriswest.info.

Want to learn more?

nlp school **europe**

Get your new NLP knowledge truly 'in the muscle' by taking part in a training course with Robbie Steinhouse.

The courses are a rich, effective and enjoyable learning experience. You'll come away with insights and tools you can apply both at work and in the rest of your life – to sales, negotiation, entrepreneurship, deal-making, self-starting, planning and leadership; to self-awareness, relationships, health and positive thinking.

All of the change processes in this book are taught on our NLP training programmes.

To join an NLP training course or to arrange an in-house training, visit www.nlpschool.com.

Index

adapted child 120–2, 125
  healing 153–4
administration
  repetitive tasks 36–7
  skills 40
advice
  from mentors 21–2, 24
  from professionals 22–4
  gleaning 20–2
  sources of 23–4
  tips 21, 22
advisors 49, 82
  anchoring role of 57, 58
anchoring 53–5
  gestures 54–5
  I-D-EA-S process 55–8, 59
  images, places and sound 55
angel investors 47
'as if' frame 96, 97, 156
assessing staff 113–16
  assessment form 173–4
assets 80, 81–2, 171
  financial 80, 82
  human 80, 81, 82
  intellectual 80, 81, 82
  physical 80, 81, 82

Bandler, Richard 5, 67
bank, relationship with 46–7
bankruptcy 63–4
Bateson, Gregory 5, 100, 144

behaviourism 77
behaviours 75, 76
Belbin, Meredith 115
beliefs 2, 62–6, 73–4, 76, 90
  being the boss 110–12
Berne, Eric 6, 119, 122–3, 152,
    155
blockages 26
body language 51, 52–3
boss, being the 110–12
  and partners 119
bottlenecks 145–6
Branson, Richard 45
Burch, Noel 20
business
  boutique 130–1
  as cash cow 132, 149
  growth or not 131
  having a life 152–60
  leaving on a high 141–3
  making it nicer 131–2
  niche 131
  staying small 130–1
  taking more out 132
  See also growth of business
business coaching see coaching
business partners 118–19, 128
  complementary skills 118, 119
business plan, five-minute 14, 15

Campbell, Joseph 24–5, 29